An Introduction to Wooden Boat Building

AN INTRODUCTION TO WOODEN BOAT BUILDING

Always More to Learn

Thad Danielson

COPYRIGHT © 2020 Thad Danielson

All rights reserved

ISBN: 978-0-9856501-5-5
Points East Publishing, Inc.

CONTENTS

PREFACE
    Boat Building   1

INTRODUCTION
    Fundamentals of Boatbuilding   11
    Designs   13
    Lofting   15
    Setting Up   18
    Materials   19
    Tools   20

NORWEGIAN PRAM –
CLINKER BUILDING BY EYE   23

ARTHUR SPURLING ROWBOAT --
Built as any other Boat can be
From Plans with Offsets   45
    Lofting the Spurling Rowboat   53
    Patterning for Spurling
        Rowboat Construction   61
    Boatbuilding   68

OARS   104

WENCE THIS INTEREST IN BOATS
AND BOATBUILDING? AND ABOUT
BEING FORTUNATE IN MY FRIENDS   106

GLOSSARY   122

PREFACE

BOAT BUILDING

Building a boat is not an endeavor to be undertaken lightly, but it is one of the most rewarding possible. I have a friend who was an auto mechanic, mostly building and maintaining race cars, but when his wife got cancer, he became watcher and care giver. He turned to boat building for his own therapy, using his car lift as support for his boat, his creative response to distress. We don't need that kind of stress to inspire an interest in building boats. The desire to get out on the water has lead many who don't want to buy a plastic production boat to build stitch and glue plywood, strip plank or plywood kit boats. The satisfaction gained from building these boats is evident in hearing tales of the building process as well as cruises made possible.

Boat building, restoration and handling has become very useful for many people with problems, young and old. There are boat building programs in many major cities for young people finding difficulty coping with their lives. There are restoration and sailing programs with returning military with PTSD. In these programs the craft of handling wood and tools, requiring concentration and developing skill, is most important to success, and these programs are very successful. Almost all for these programs focus on traditional wooden boats.

Traditional wooden boats have personality that comes from the wood, the builder and the designer. The builder is attached to the boat as a living thing created by his or her hands. Different woods are used for different parts of a boat depending on the character of each type of wood. Different tools are wanted for the different operations needed to fashion pieces of wood into the parts that go into the boat. You keep the tools in working condition and use them so they do the work required, you being just the handler, the tool being the worker. This may seem the Zen of boat building but it makes boat building satisfying, that and seeing the boat in it's element at the end.

My own interest in building boats came mostly from a desire to get out to sea. Growing up, I had crossed oceans in ships and watched boats of all kinds handled in all kinds of conditions. The boat handlers were craftsmen handling craft built by craftsmen. Sail and paddle dugout canoes, sculled and rowed open boats, sailing yachts, motor launches, tug boats, ships, their functional shapes and their handling was wonderful. So, this was my interest in boats, that, and enjoying every chance I had to be in a boat. Seeing the beauty of boats and appreciating the skill of their crews was well and good, but seeing the structure of a boat in plan was it's own revelation. A beautiful sheer line, a proud prow or the curl of water from the stem underway, are easy to appreciate, but, even when inside, much is hidden of the structure that holds the boat together and gives it it's capability in the sea way. This was worth learning about, and learning to do better and better.

I have always built traditional boats out of sawn lumber. One day a man came to me saying he wanted a boat built but he wanted it strip built with epoxied glass inside and out. I said I liked the boat he wanted but not the building method, but I said I was working with a man who had built such a boat for himself, so maybe we could do that. When I spoke to my friend he said, somewhat to my surprise, "not a good idea". He said, yes, the strips go together fast, but then there are weeks of fairing to get smooth surfaces for the glass and then there is the mess of the epoxy to deal with. Also, he said, when he had worked at Dion's yard he had seen all the boats they cared for, traditionally built, when there was a problem anywhere in those boats, any part could be replaced and the boat would be as good as new. So, he said, I don't think we should do that. For all these reasons, including carrying on the skills that characterize much of human life over the last thousands of years, I recommend building a boat.

I've been teaching a course called Fundamentals of Boatbuilding (FOB) at the WoodenBoat School (WBS) in Brooklin, Maine, for a few years now. The first year I asked what I should do, how does this go? The answer came that there were a variety of boats there in various stages of construction from previous classes and the class could work on my choice from those. The main idea was to have one lapstrake/clinker boat and one carvel, to acquaint the class with these two types of traditional hull construction.

The shop at the WoodenBoat School is the old barn building on the estate that is now home to WoodenBoat magazine. I believe some cows were kept on the estate, but this building is all brick and concrete, not at all a typical barn and fitting it's present use very well. FOB classes are given in the room at the far left end with two big sliding door openings.

The old estate barn, now home to the WoodenBoat School. Fundamentals of Boatbuilding classes have the near end with the two big sliding door openings, probably the former carriage house.

I came with a box of tools and my sharpening kit, finding a Chaisson dory skiff ready for planking (clinker) and a couple of Catspaw dinghies, one all planked ready for finishing, the other ready for planking. On the lofting table was lofting for the Catspaw, Joel White's 12' carvel variation on Herreshoff's Columbia lifeboat model dinghy. There were other options but I stuck with those. The class was full with eleven students aged 20 to 73 and equally wide range of experience from none to having built a number of stitch and glue boats. The latter came for experience with traditional clinker methods and materials.

Almost before we introduced ourselves I was asked to check out some planes and chisels that didn't work, leading to sharpening demonstrations with happy results. Sharp knives cut, so might as well start with sharpening, but, after introductions and a little talk about my plan for the class, we went on to lofting. What we had was the lofting on the table which I talked about, but there was nothing there really for us to do but see and try to understand how it related to the boats on the other side of the room. On to the jobs at hand, the class split itself up into groups (changeable over the course of time to some extent) based on interest, and went to work.

This was all well and good, but I still had no notion of what would happen in subsequent years, what MY class would be like. Here we were, trying to do a good job working on other people's boats, learning about the tools, materials and techniques involved with building wooden boats, fine. In the back of my mind was always the question about where I would go with this WoodenBoat School business. That was about to change.

A few days into the class a small group came to me asking if we could do a lofting, so they could see a lofting done. Lofting is taking sets of numbers called offsets, because they are measurements of distance off a centerline or baseline (Cartesian coordinates, essentially), drawing the corresponding grid, making marks at the measured points and drawing fair lines through the marks. Because the original numbers were measured on a small scale drawing or carved model, seldom will all the offsets in a table of offsets produce the desired fair lines, and fair smooth curves are most important for the look and function of the vessel as well as for elements of the boats structure to work together. Lofting then is a process, after the basic grid is laid down, of taking the given numbers, seeing if they produce fair lines in the boats full size, and making adjustments so that all four two dimensional "views" lofted form a consistent image with all lines fair. Both the steps of the process and the basis for making decisions need to be well thought out.

One of the boats I have owned and sailed was a John G. Alden designed Triangle sloop. The design was drawn in 1925 and the first 5 boats came out in 1926. My boat was built in 1927. In 1928 there was a fire at the James Graves Yacht Yard that burned up the building mold for Triangles. With more orders in hand for this sweet sailing 28' knockabout, a new mold was built based on a new lofting and the newer boats were always a little different from the old. David Hooks, who worked for Alden and whose family had owned Triangles, said he thought maybe Clifford Swain, who drew the plan for Alden, and liked a sharp entry, had supervised the original lofting at Graves yard, while Aage Nielsen, who liked full bows, had supervised the later lofting – accounting for the difference between the two productions.

I was glad to have had this request and went looking for a plan that would serve, not taking too long to lay down. I went through the books of small boat designs put together by John Gardner, published by Mystic Seaport Museum, where he had been curator of small craft, and found what I was looking for in his article on Arthur Spurling rowboats. The plan shown seemed made for lofting in one day, but it isn't for an Arthur Spurling boat. Gardner says the plan is like the Spurling and that someone should measure one of the Spurling boats. The school staff produced painted plywood overnight, which we fastened to the lofting table, lofting out the lines the next day. I hope the students who worked on the lofting learned something, but John Gardner's words gave me the start needed to develop my own Fundamentals of Boatbuilding class.

That class got the dory skiff planked and ribbed with some other interior structure, the one Catspaw was almost completely planked and the other completed. The class did well with this makeshift situation, enjoying themselves and learning too. When the school director asked if I wanted to teach the next year, and what I thought to do, I said I thought I'd try to get together plans for the Spurling rowboat, build that and a built by eye Norwegian pram. Sounds good, he said.

I began with research and inquiring among friends. I heard from Ben Fuller at the Penobscot Maritime Museum in Searsport, Maine, that both Ralph Stanley and his son Richard had measured boats they cared for and built to their plans, also that the PMM had a Spurling that we might use. He also spoke of David Cockey who uses photographs fed into a computer program to develop plans from existing vessels. A Spurling 12' rowboat was in Mystic Seaport Museum's collection, accession #1985.79. Inquiring, Mystic did not have plans and this boat had never been measured for plans. Having been put on this job by John Gardner, this boat called for attention. Telling another former curator of small craft at Mystic, Peter Vermilya, about this project, he said the first time he was at Northeast Harbor, Mount Desert Island, Maine, there were a string of Spurling rowboats at the float. He took one out and it gave him a whole new perspective on rowing! This was high praise.

I think Peter Vermilya told me who to talk to at Mystic but David Cockey may have made the contact first. By working with the Mystic legal department and the volunteers who take care of the boat collection we got a date to meet and measure the Spurling, David with his camera and me with plumb bob, levels, rulers, paper and pencil.

Spurling rowboat set up at Mystic Seaport for measurement

Philip Tankard and his group of volunteers had the boat off her rack and set up for the big job. Peter Vermilya and a few other interested observers stood around as David took hundreds of pictures from many angles, the more the merrier. I did get a chance to make some measurements, but mostly I got to look her over for details. One detail stuck out, the keel is doubled with a shoe, both 8 inches wide amidship. This interested me because the plan Gardner's book shows as like the Spurling has a plank on edge keel and for a dinghy rowing around the islands of Maine with their rocky beaches and concrete landing ramps, the flat wide keel, doubled, made perfect sense and really made this boat very different in use from the plan in the book.

Spurling rowboat showing broad oak shoe, as set up in the Mystic Seaport collection building for measurement.

After that first visit I went back 4 times, refining my measurement technique and recording more details. I couldn't pull screws or cut into the boat so I had to call Richard Stanley to ask about the skeg material, "cedar with an oak shoe", good man. Floorboards made it impossible to see what happens on top of the keel, but then I got an iPad with the camera lens right in the corner making it possible with a flashlight to see and record the way the ribs land on the keel. In the end I was pleased with my lines and the construction drawing, presenting a copy to Mystic Seaport as agreed.

Cedar skeg and oak sternpost detail showing cedar keel and oak shoe with bronze/brass heel bracket. These photos of Arthur Spurling rowboat in Mystic Seaport collection.

I had built a few Norwegian prams by eye. L. Francis Herreshoff says, when he had sailed to England in one of his father's schooners, these prams were popular tenders and he rowed one from the Isle of Wight almost across the Solent and back, seeming to find that a great recommendation. Beside their capabilities, pram building by eye is very direct and instructive. The hull is constructed first, with plank shapes and the angles between the planks creating the shape. Traditional Norwegian prams had sawn frames but we steam bend ribs after fitting transoms in the ends. Relatively straight grained wood bends in fair curves and bending such planks with fair curved edges produces a good looking boat, good rowing and towing boat too.

Prams are clinker/lapstrake boats with transoms at both ends, ideally the bow transom quite small. In stem and transom clinker boats, the riveted, beveled, laps hold the hull shape, but fastening to backbone structure at the ends masks the strength and structure built into the lapped plank hull. Building prams by eye it's almost magical how the boat's shape develops, if you don't understand it, you see and feel it. Then you row it, after the other parts are fitted and installed. I like these things about the pram as teaching tool, but I also like that pram building this way is a procedure more than a plan and with different conceptions the procedure will produce different boats, each functional and handsome.

So, here we go with how to build the Norwegian pram by eye and the Spurling rowboat from plans. The pram's lapstrake/clinker hull built following the classic procedure. The Spurling's carvel hull lofted and built with ribbanded molds just as you would build a much larger boat to plan. We will lay down a grid and loft the Spurling. We will bend a pram bottom board and start planking. We will cut, bevel and rabbet the Spurling backbone, construct station molds and secure them in place, before bending ribbands around and bending ribs to the ribbands. The pram planked up, transoms will get shaped and installed in the ends before ribs are milled out, steamed, bent in and riveted in place. Pairs of planks for the Spurling will be spiled for, got out and fastened. Both boats will need their share of knees, risers, thwarts, floorboards, and other finishing details. Here we go, but first I will start with the little thing handed out to the class before we start.

INTRODUCTION

FUNDAMENTALS OF BOATBUILDING, Introduction for My Class

If you don't start, you won't finish.

"No boat was ever built with wood you don't have" -- Pete Culler

Speaking of material needs for boat building, there are more or less ideal conditions as well as making do with what you have. Most boat buildings combine these options in one way or another. For thousands of years boats were built with stone ax and adze the only tools. With metal working, both tool and fastening options expanded, but still in living memory many boats were built with little more tools than an ax. My own experience suggests that you will use every tool you can get your hands on, whether it is a hatchet or a shop full of power tools. Likewise for wood, every species available will get considered whether useable or not. Most boat plans call for particular woods for different parts of the vessel. Building in a particular location, the particular stock list may not be available, but it will suggest woods with their attributes, long with straight grain, tough and curved, light or heavy. Fasteners present similar issues of access, cost and preference.

Fundamentally, work with a building method and design that compliments available skills and resources. All the above is easy to understand, such as it is, but like everything else it is all in the details. Wherever your interest in boats comes from, we all start from somewhere in the spectrum of interest and knowledge. Talking to Gerald Smith, Marblehead boat builder, yacht captain and decoy carver at least 85 years old at the time, he spoke one day of learning something about his craft that day. In businesses like these there is always more to learn, no matter where we start, and it's all fun.

Boats of all kinds from skiffs to ocean liners are complex integrated structures having similar parts scaled to their different sizes. Looking at boats and using boats can inspire interest and appreciation without identifying the different elements that make up the structure. In boat design and construction, seaworthiness is surely paramount, at least for the waters of intended use. The boat builder needs to have the end result in mind throughout the building process as well as the process itself, defining the shapes of all the boats different parts, producing the parts and fastening them together. Wherever we start in describing the building process it becomes obvious that familiarity with the language of boat building is important. Glossaries of boat building terms and nautical dictionaries might help, but regional variations and varying definitions will appear in spite of remarkable consistency among the world's many languages and cultures.

"There are no problems, only solutions" -- Lee Van Gemert quoting his boat builder grandfather.

The boat builder's problems are similar whatever the design, culture or location, thus the universality of boat terms. Solutions, however, vary widely -- there's always more to learn. Look at plans drawn by different designers and you see wide variations in level of construction detail and specification. Some plans show little more than the lines, usually with a sketch of interior arrangements. A few show close detail of nearly every joint and construction element. Even with this level of detail the designer relies on the boat builder to know how to fashion the parts and fasten properly. Wood being an organic material, sharp tools and constant attention to your work yield good results, with more than a little help from memory and imagination.

DESIGNS

Until the middle of the 19th Century most boat designs existed in the builder's head and perhaps in a midship section outline on the shop floor, many handed on from one generation to the next ("midship section outline" becomes in boat design and building terminology "midship station in body plan"). My father once built a boat with a friend of his that I never saw in the water, for two reasons somewhat related: Built of exceptionally heavy wood it was not easy to get it to the water just across the street, but the wood being also very strong and not yet stable, the keel took a curve as they built, producing a boat that went in circles. Gondolas are built asymmetrical as they are rowed from one side only, the shape countering the oars turning force. Since we want most boats to go straight until we want to turn, boat designs are done as half models with the two sides then built as mirror images.

Many boats have been built using carved half-models. Nathanael Greene Herreshoff designed all his boats carving half-models from white pine blocks. He measured the half-models mechanically and expanded the measurements arithmetically to define shapes of molds to build on and for drawings showing construction and layout details. According to his son, L. Francis (CAPT. NAT HERRESHOFF, The Wizard of Bristol, p. 129 in my paperback copy) Capt. Nat started with a sketch showing the general idea, used to define the basic dimensions and shape (midship section included), then with a block of the right size he would carve until he had the shape he wanted. Probably most designers, whatever the design method, start with a sketch of some sort. Designs done at the drafting table are done with lines drawings.

All of N. G. Herreshoff's designs were done for construction in his own shops under his supervision. A set of plans from any other source will include Lines drawings, Construction and Layout drawings, sail plan (for sailboats) and a Table of Offsets. The plan set should also include a sheet detailing scantlings and materials, though these are often shown as notes on the construction drawings. The lines drawings are Body Plan, Profile, Half-breadth, and Diagonals. All these drawings are, of course, two dimensional. A half-hull carved model will have a flat side representing a vertical plane that would divide the symmetrical hull in half between the stem and stern, in the plan set this is called the Center Line (CL). Lengthwise along the center line the hull drawings are divided into numbered Stations, square to the center line. Sometimes these stations will correspond to frame locations in the construction drawings, sometimes not.

The Body Plan shows the hull shape in cross section at each station with forward stations on one side of the center line and aft stations on the other side. On a Body Plan drawing there will be vertical lines parallel to the centerline, horizontal lines square to the centerline and diagonal lines from the centerline out through the body lines, the buttocks, waterlines and diagonals, respectively.

The Profile drawing then shows the hull profile along the center line (plane), the buttocks parallel to the centerline and curved, including the sheer and backbone profiles. The waterlines and stations appear as straight lines on the Profile drawing. Some details such as ballast and rabbet lines should also be shown in this drawing. One of the waterlines might be the design Load Water Line (LWL), and there is often a baseline from which offsets are measured though sometimes offsets are measured above and below the LWL.

The Half-Breadth (HB) drawing shows the half-outline of the hull where it intersects with the horizontal waterlines, as well as half-breadth of sheer and keel. Centerline, buttocks and stations appear as straight lines on this drawing.

The Diagonal drawing is based on the diagonals on the body plan with the length of diagonal from centerline to hull at each station connected full length, here only the centerline, stations and diagonals are shown. Drawn generally as planks run and as water moves along the hull under way, fair is most important with diagonals both in design and lofting.

Looking through boat designs, mostly people will concentrate on profile drawings and accommodations, these show her looks and set up for intended use. With a design chosen, the builder needs the construction drawing to develop materials lists. Building starts with accumulating materials and lofting, drawing out the lines drawings full size.

LOFTING

To draw full size requires a floor a little bigger than the boat to come, also pencils, battens, weights or awls to hold battens in desired positions, and measuring devises. Traditional battens are straight grain pine, flexible, making even, fair curves. Many other batten materials can be used. Pine works easily and I often plane different parts of battens to make them more flexible where the design calls for tighter curves. For all lines "fair" is the word, meaning a smooth, even curve with no flat or hard spots, no sharp bends. Molds set up for building must be fair in the sense that planks bent around the molds must be able to land on each mold in turn. Likewise round sided and round bottom boats need to be fair from sheer to keel, or sheer to chine and chine to keel. Having battens that easily take fair curves helps a lot when lofting but the eye is still most important in adjusting the batten for fair, to best realize the intended shape.

Boat plans are generally scaled at 1" to 1', 1 in 12. I expect designers working in metric would often use 1 in 10, still in the same reduction range. To expand a design to full size in lofting, we take measurements taken from a drawing or a model multiplied by whatever factor to attain full size offsets, mark them on grids accurately scaled up from the design drawing, centerlines, buttocks, waterlines, and diagonals, and draw fair lines connecting the appropriate marks. Fair is more important than hitting all the marks.

Drafted with pencil or ink on paper a line might be a 50th of an inch wide, expanded by a factor of 12, this would be almost 1/4th of an inch wide. Establishing the point at which two such lines intersect at right angles can be fairly accurately done but when intersections are more or less oblique it becomes more difficult. Near to right angle with the hull lines, diagonal offsets are more trusted in lofting than buttock and waterline offsets. With design done on such small scale, lofting is needed to assure a fair boat from beginning to end of construction. For carvel, smooth skin, boats especially, whatever foundation is set up based on the lofting must allow fair tight landing for the planks. So we loft, deciding along the way how to weight divergent offsets from the offset table, producing a lofting with all the lines agreeing on the loft floor, assured they will come together on the hull to come, as accurately as possible matching the designers design.

With the lines lofted we come to lofting's second purpose, patterning the basic structural components for building. This will include backbone elements, showing joints and fastenings, as well as mold shapes upon which planking will land to produce the designed vessel. For inboard powered vessels the shaft line will be established as shown in plan, with floor and engine beds drawn to assure that everything can fit. With planking coming to the backbone at different angles from stem to stern, the lofting is also used to determine bevels for plank landings. Because these angles are different throughout most boats, bevel angles are measured at regular intervals along the backbone so bevels and rabbets can be cut at these locations and fairly joined. For Transom vessels, the lofting is used to determine the inside and outside true shape of the transom, producing the transom bevels. On sawn framed vessels where the frames are the building molds, the frames are generally set up square to the centerline, parallel to or on station lines, so their outside faces must be beveled for plank landing. These bevels also come from the lofting in a process just curious enough to confuse.

Back in high school geometry a line square to a line or surface was called normal to the line or surface, curious, but OK, just a word. But learning to loft and build boats, "normal" makes lots of sense both with how boat parts are designed on the loft floor and how they are made in the shop. Cutting a bevel with chisel or bandsaw we cut normal to the piece, frame, stem or keel. The body plan and the mold shapes developed from a lofting provide the keel bevels but we need the lofting to determine stem rabbet bevels. We need to know the angle of bevel normal to the piece at regular locations along the stem, not the angle to waterline or buttock, or the angle of the plank. On the Profile drawing we pick out a few representative spots along the stem. At each one a line is drawn normal to the curve at that point, that is, square to the tangent of the point on the curve. This defines a plane through the hull. Where the line crosses each waterline we draw lines square off our line. Moving to the Half-breadth drawing we measure the half-breadth of the hull at these points of intersection and mark them on their respective waterlines. Drawing the stem half breadth to the rabbet beside our centerline, we join the waterline half-breadths with a fair line to the rabbet half breadth giving us the hull body plan normal to the stem rabbet at that point. The angle between the stem side at the rabbet and the hull/planking as drawn is the rabbet bevel we need to cut at that point.

Few have trouble setting up a design's lofting grid, marking offsets on the grid and drawing fair lines through (or near) the marked points. Many have trouble determining bevel angles. I hope this helps see how this works and why we need to know these angles.

Of course, as in every aspect of this business, there are many solutions to every problem and different traditions. The method described above gives a directly useful result that can be cut on the bench, or at the bandsaw if a frame. Many a bevel however has been cut in place after the backbone and molds are set up. Battens can be bent around the molds and bevels worked with planes and chisels, or adze for larger vessels.

SETTING UP

Different designs call for different set ups and most traditional designs don't include a specified approach to building. Final results are specified but achieving those results is up to the builder, even when a method is suggested. Upside down or right side up. Ladder frame, solid floor, strong-back, few molds or many, or none, molds ribbanded or not, there are many options. Different designs suggest different set ups. In traditional clinker or lapstrake construction, riveting plank laps before installing interior framework is easy built right side up and difficult built upside down. Herreshoff Manufacturing Company's method was to always build upside down on the boat's own framework secured to molds, ensuring control of the final shape. For screw fastened carvel hulls this was one thing, for lapstrake dinghies, of which they built hundreds, this may have made fitting easier in places but called for temporary fastenings in many places and riveting after the hull was right side up and off the molds.

Whatever set up style we pick, accuracy in set up makes successful building possible. Designs are usually drawn with waterlines level, stations square to the waterlines and (in the construction drawings) frame timbers parallel to station lines. Pulling mold shapes off the lofting parallel to the stations, the molds need careful set up, plumb and square to centerline, spaced accurately as planned. Once carefully located to your satisfaction the molds must be securely braced and cross braced so they won't move as building proceeds.

MATERIALS

Back to Pete Culler's statement about building with available materials. It's all very well to say you can't build with what you don't have, but you want a boat that will last, last at least long enough to get you to shore. Also, boat building is labor intensive and we don't want to waste our time, for this reason, also, it pays to find materials that have the right qualities for boat parts. Unfortunately many small manufacturers have gone out of business in recent year and mass marketing dominates. The relatively small and wide-spread wooden boat building community depends on similarly small and widespread suppliers for much of it's needs. While most established sawmills still working are cutting short stock dimensional lumber, there are some still interested in specialty markets, like wooden boats. Also, there are people with portable band mills all over this country and others who do custom sawing. Talk to sawyers and foresters, they know where the wood is, logs, lumber or trees that might fit your needs. Many of these people are interested in the boat builder's particular needs and they know wood. I have always enjoyed this part of boat building, finding sources of lumber, talking to sawyers and lumber dealers, looking at trees.

Plans for wooden boats will usually include timber specifications for the different structural elements. Sometimes this will be a separate list and sometimes spread around the construction plan drawing(s). A stock list taken from plans will generally be for boat building timber in common use in the designers or builder's locale, or in the case of historical documentation where the original boat was built. Without access to the designers listed timber, knowledge of available woods and their characteristics will be important, matching weight, strength and rot resistance being most important. We always want air dry or green timber. For floors and other structural parts where little flexibility is required, and inboard joinery, kiln dried stock can be used, though kiln drying methods are not always best for wood which will live with a boat's damp conditions and seaway stresses.

With wood must also come fasteners. Backbone timbers, patterned from lofting and carefully shaped with faying surfaces painted, must be bolted together. Planks, spiled for and got out of waiting boards, must be secured to timbers. For price and longevity only wooden through nails (trenails) compete with copper rivets and headed bolts. These through fastenings require backing (in many cases a two person job), so screws and threaded bolts are more widely used. In many cases steel screws and bolts have been the fasteners of choice because of price and availability, but rust destroys the fasteners and the wood around them, especially quick in salt water. Silicon Bronze has become the most common material for these fasteners today, being free of lead and zinc. Many people are attracted to stainless steel, but stainless steels are around half iron and in the presence of moving salt water they loose material where starved of oxygen, where you can't see what is happening -- not good. Other materials like monel are good but either very expensive or unavailable. So the usual choice is between copper and silicon bronze.

TOOLS

"You never have enough tools" or "there's always another tool you need", and "you can always use more clamps" -- comments and thoughts like these are common enough but, as said before, many boats have been built with little more tools than a hatchet. Apart from clamps and fastening tools (ball peen hammers, screw drivers, wrenches and the like), most boat building tools are cutting tools, planes, chisels, and saws being most common.

Cutting tools work best when sharp, with some woods only really sharp edges will cut as you need to cut. So, you need to know sharp from dull and how to sharpen. Sharp, for me, is two polished surfaces meeting. If you look straight on at the edge you should see reflection on the polished faces but no reflection on the edge, no edge at all. Little nicks show up sparkling on the edge. Flat or turned edges reflect, they also won't cut. Not only will a sharp edge cut but it will stay sharp.

Severely damaged edges call for serious grinding, preferably on a rough fast-cutting stone. High speed grinders rapidly heat the ground metal, especially the thin edge of the wedge, and the tool must be frequently cooled in water or oil to maintain temper. Better not to use these machines but sometimes it seems the only way. Temper is the hardness level of the tool that controls ability to sharpen and keep an edge in use.

Many different sharpening systems exist. Many years ago I was in the Woodcraft store looking at a Japanese waterstone, 6000 grit gold stone, on their clearance table. A man also looking at the table said I should buy it, he had one already or he would have bought it, you work the surface with water and the nagura stone to create a slurry that is the cutting/polishing medium, don't wash the slurry off, he said. I bought it and that stone still works. Those 6000 and 8000 grit stones polish beautifully for a fine edge. Japanese waterstones come in a wide range of grits all of which work in the same way, with nagura raised slurry. Arkansas natural stones use either water or oil to carry metal particles away and come in varying grades as well. There are also systems that use pastes and compounds containing particles with different cutting and polishing qualities. These usually use a sheet of glass as a base for the compound. Like me, most people probably use the system they learned first, but the object is the same, polished face meets polished face, the edge disappearing, sharp.

A sharp knife (chisel, plane iron, etc) will stay sharp in use but will dull eventually. Different woods dull a blade faster at different rates. Very hard woods take their toll and others, especially tropical hardwoods, contain pockets of stony secretions that are unavoidable. Working on a job you start to notice the need to work harder or you start to get tear out instead of a clean cut, it's time to sharpen.

There is one rule, like all rules there are exceptions taken at your own risk, the rule is: Never have any part of your body in front of the knife.

Tools sharp, time to start.

NORWEGIAN PRAM, CLINKER BUILDING BY EYE

Pram built by WoodenBoat School class in 2016

Norwegian prams come in two classes, Holmsbru and Arendal, the former with the bottom board under the garboards, the latter with the garboards underneath and a shoe fitted under the bottom board between the garboard edges. The building process is the same but I land the garboards on top the bottom board to simplify the process. With the bottom board at the bottom I want it heavier than the rest of the planking to take the shocks and scrapes of landing. Pram building starts with shaping a bottom board and springing it to give plenty of rocker. Rocker in the bottom board is needed to produce the shape and pleasing sheer we are after. At the School we have been using pine for planking though one year we used eastern cedar for the bottom board, a heavier wood like oak would be fine.

Bottom Board Shape and Setup

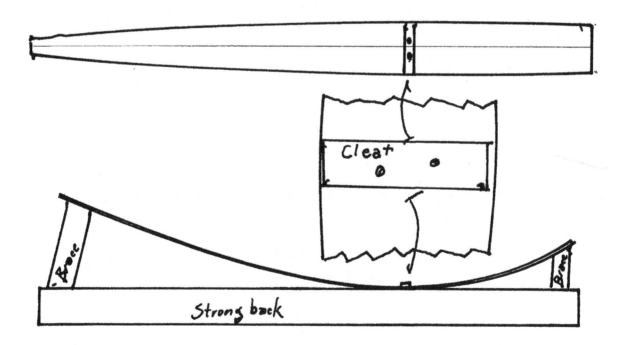

To spring rocker into the bottom board we need a strongback holding it down a little aft of the middle and stakes at each end holding the ends up. We will be riveting the garboards to the bottom's edges, so we need a strongback a little narrower than the bottom, at least 2 inches narrower. At WBS we use a 2 x 6 strongback at least as long as the boat will be, say 12'. When we hold the bottom board down to the strongback and lift the ends for rocker, a 2 x 6 will be bent up in the middle, reducing the induced rocker, unless we either put a brace up to the ceiling or stiffen the strongback, maybe with a 2 x 4 on edge fastened underneath. I have also used a heavier timber that wouldn't need bracing. Set up the strongback a little more than knee high, on sawhorses.

Bottom board set up for pram building. Cleat holding board down to strongback plank with ends braced up on block with clearance for fastening planks.

The WBS has supplied ½ inch pine for pram planking, 10 inches wide. For the bottom board, I would like 1 inch, 4/4, but have made do with 3/4". Deciding on the bottom board shape and cutting it out begins the building process. Our laps will be around 1 inch wide, so the bow end of the bottom board can't be less than 2 inches across, 1 inch half breadth. We want the middle to be as wide as our stock allows. The stern should be a little narrower than the middle, but wider than the bow end. With a board in hand, we need to mark a centerline on the board and have a batten to bend for marking plank edges. As with all our wood choices, we want to make the best use of the chosen board, avoiding knots, following grain, limiting rot-prone sapwood, and this starts with drawing the centerline. With a centerline drawn we mark a bow width, stern width, and spring our batten on one side from these marks to the widest spot. Spring clamps make holding and adjusting the batten easy. As the center of displacement will be aft of the middle we might put the widest point of this first plank there but we might also push the batten a little wider than it may want further forward, always watching to see that the curve achieved is fair. When satisfied with the line produced, we draw the line on the one side, flip the batten to the other side, adjusting it to match the first line, and draw that line.

After picking and lining out the bottom board we cut it out. I like to cut with a circular saw, supporting the board on sticks laid across a stiff plank. Moving the saw, supported by the wood being cut, and staying outside the line, but close, is easier than maneuvering a long piece through a band or table saw. Setting the saw blade as shallow as possible, the kerf allows you to cut surprising curves with good control as long as you keep moving forward or stop, trying to back up with the blade turning can lead to problems. After thus roughing out our plank we plane to the lines before planing to thickness, if needed, and are now prepared to spring the bottom board to shape. If we were building an Arendal pram we might be cutting lap bevels on the underside of the bottom board, but we're not doing that here.

I make up posts to support the ends from 2 x 4 stock. The bow post around 14" high, the stern, 5". I cut bevels for the top to suggest the angle on which the board end will land, then on the bow post I trim the edges to leave only a ¼ to ½ inch ridge to support the board. With the new bottom board lying on the strongback we drill through a short cleat and the bottom board on the centerline about 2/3ds of the way aft and securely fasten to the strongback with screw or bolt, the cleat across the board, with space at each end to land the garboard lap. At this time a brace could be run to the ceiling to hold the bottom board down before the ends are lifted. Lifting the ends, we see if we can lift enough to set the prepared posts under the ends. When all is well, we toe nail (with screws) the posts to the strongback and put screws through the bottom board into the tops of the posts. Now we're ready for planking.

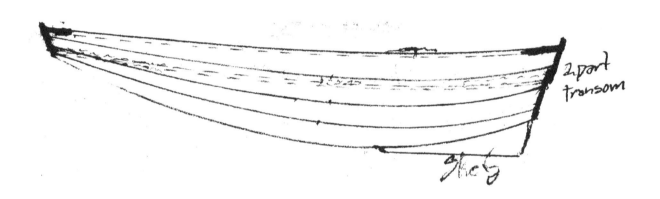

Basic pram shape.

My first pram on the ramp for a river row.

For the first pram I built, I followed the directions in the article by Arne Emil Christensen in WoodenBoat volume 46 from 1982, using the measured drawing he shows. Nine feet long and very round in sections, it was tippy to board but manageable when seated, oars in the water, and small. When first launched, I rowed out to a boat in the harbor that I knew flew a Norwegian flag and showed "Oslo" for hale on the transom. It was evening and light showed through the cabin ports. I shouted "ahoy" and knocked on the hull. Anders came into the cockpit and, looking over the side, exclaimed, "I never saw a smaller one!" to lead off the conversation. His family had a 14' pram in Norway, etc., every few minutes he'd say "That's very small" or something else to that effect. It was really, at best, a one person boat. Years later I met Mark Swanson who was featured building prams in that same WoodenBoat issue and described my experience. He said he had had the same experience and that was the way with that plan. But! the experience was not really about the particular boat, it was about the process of building prams by eye.

All boats are integrated structures made up of relatively weak parts linked by relatively weak joints creating amazingly strong wholes. The pram and the rowboat we are building are examples of two types of construction, clinker/lapstrake and carvel/smooth skin. In carvel construction, planks are not fastened to each other but to an interior framing structure, the planks carefully fitted tight to each other or with caulking, held tight to the framework by their fasteners, keeping the water out. In clinker construction, the planks are fastened together along their edges, the planks at angles to each other determined by bevels cut along the plank edges. This creates a form of unibody construction where the interior framework is supportive both of the plank structure and interior fittings, but the planks form a stable structure themselves. In clinker planking, we spile to establish the shape of the joining edge of the new plank with the angle the new plank will take to what is there, and then we bevel the lower plank edge to set the new plank at the desired angle when fastened in place. For fasteners we use copper rivets, copper nails driven through drilled holes, through a burr/rove, before being cut off and peened over the burr/rove, clamping the joint tight.

    The first step in getting out a plank is called spiling, which is defined as establishing the shape of a curve. The bottom board edges were cut in curves drawn to a batten but planks above the garboards are likely to come to that curve at an angle and perhaps twisting at different angles, thus having a different shape. In lapstrake building we tend to use the actual plank for spiling, though if you will be resawing a thick board to get out matching planks you need to use a separate piece as a spiling batten. To build a pram with more initial stability than that little one I first built we want the garboards to lie parallel with the bottom board, or nearly so, through the body of the boat with perhaps a little twist up coming to the bow. To spile we clamp plank stock to the bottom board, holding it at the angle we want, and draw a line along the edge of the bottom board, giving the shape of the garboard's lower edge. You might remember that we need to allow for the inch lap, which can be taken into account by drawing a line 1 inch from the bottom board edge and keeping the spiling batten covering that line to leave stock in the new plank for the lap. In any case that line is useful when the plank gets fastened in place. Because your line might be a little rough it is good to redraw with a batten and if your batten is just under 1 inch wide then you can draw lines on both sides, defining the plank edge and lap width.

With a line drawn for the lower edge of the plank we cut and plane to the line. If we are going to resaw, for matching planks, this is done full thickness for the full plank shape. Next we spring a batten to define the upper edge of the new planks. Again we want the bow to be as small as possible and the stern a little narrower than amidship where we want as much width as we can get out of our stock, <u>most important is to have a fair line</u>. With our stock fully shaped, now is the time to use it as template for the opposite side or to resaw. If the garboard is to have a little bevel along it's length, to lift it from the bottom board plane (deadrise) and twist at the bow end, now is the time to plane a bevel along the lower inside edge with added "gain" toward the bow. Note that we are likely to have to steam the bow end of the plank to achieve any desired twist but this will only be successful if building with air dry wood, not kiln dried. Gain is cut with a rabbet plane against a stop marking the lap edge, bevel needs to be cut flat without any hump in the middle and a changing bevel needs to be planed with a rolling bevel, no sharp changes allowed. To cut bevels on plank edges, we have a line at the 1 inch lap line, and then we place a straight edge hard to the plank edge at the desired bevel angle, noting how far the straight edge stands away from the lap line – transferring that distance to the plank edge and running it along the edge as long as that bevel is maintained we now have two lines to plane to for our bevel.

Next we need to decide on the bevel on the upper outside edge of the new planks for the plank to come. For that we need to clamp one garboard in place on the bottom board. I like to start by trying to make the lower edge of the coming plank as straight as possible. We do that by standing at the bow holding a combination square to the forward end of the plank. Look down the length of the plank and at the standing part of the square and rotate the square until the standing part, ruled straight edge, and the plank edge aline, not necessarily perfectly but noticeably. That angle will be a good angle to work with and you might as well note how much has to be taken off to create the bevel for landing the next plank. After taking the plank off, plane that bevel on both garboards and they will be ready to fasten where they belong.

I have seen some rules from an old boatbuilder for clinker fastening prescribing laps twice plank thickness and fasteners spaced six times plank thickness. With the half inch planking we have been using at WBS, my one inch lap and three inch fastener spacing schedule has been to that rule. Our fasteners are copper rivets formed from copper nails with burrs. Copper nails for riveting come "common" with round shanks and flat heads but also square shank with flat or rose heads. Holes must be drilled for the nails. In soft wood the holes should be slightly smaller than the nail shank, through hardwoods we want a press fit and too tight means the nail will bend when driving. With square shank nails a hole slightly smaller than the diagonal dimension of the shank but bigger than the square dimension is called for. Burrs are copper washers with the center hole smaller than the nail shank, roves function similarly but are thicker and have a slight cone shape. With holes drilled and nails pushed through, we use a rove set to back the burr or rove while we hammer the nail home. Rove sets are made from heavy metal with a chamfered hole to be held against the burr or rove at the nail point until the nail is driven through the burr/rove, nail head and burr/rove both tight to their respective sides of the joint. Then, as said above, the nail is cut off close above the burr/rove and peened over to form the rivet, a heavy bucking iron held against the nail head. The first couple of hammer blows should be with the flat face, spreading the nail shank in the drilled hole, followed by many light blows with the ball peen, moving around the exposed nail tip forming the rivet by mushrooming the nail end out over the burr/rove.

With the first garboard clamped securely in place we first mark for fastener placement, leaving spaces where ribs or frames will be installed later. In this case we will have a rib every 6 inches, so the initial fastener spacing will be every 6 inches. Every 9 inches with two rivets between each rib would be fine if floorboards are to be installed, otherwise closer spacing keeps feet on the timbers instead of on the planks. If using sawn frames every 30 or so inches then the rivets will be every 3 inches except where frames will be coming later.

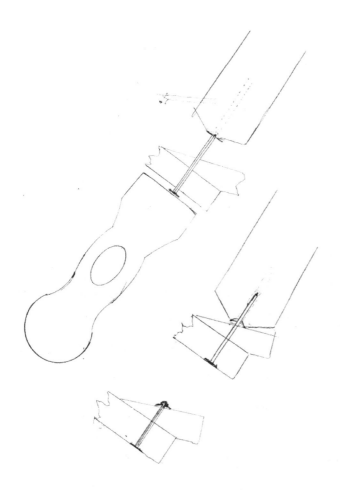

Driving the nail through the burr/rove to be cut off and riveted. Riveting, a heavy backing iron is held against the nail head, the cut off nail shank is struck a time or two with the flat peen before the ball peen is turned and used to spread the copper shank against the burr/rove. Peening is best done with many little strokes, preferably moving around the spreading end of the rivet.

Clamps for clinker construction are rather specialized but can be quite simple. I have mostly used clothespin clamps, cutting clothespin shapes out of an oak board and riveting just above the throat to prevent splitting. Slid over a plank to the joint, the ends are wedged tight. Other types of long reach clamps can be made with threaded tighteners.

Oak clothespin clamp for lapstrake/clinker boat building. Wedges tighten the clamp on plank laps.

With the plank clamped tight in place we start drilling and pushing nails through, outside to inside. Be sure you have drawn lines at the lap so the new plank is in proper position. Start at the middle and move toward the ends. The whole line of nails can be pushed through the holes before riveting begins. Again, rivet from the middle toward the ends. When one side is done, go on to the other side to finish the plank pair. Now it's ready for spiling the next plank. The process is the same as before, though now we are more concerned with making full use of the boards than with broadening the width of the bottom. Both now when spiling and also when setting the shaped plank up for fastening, if you clamp the ends and slide the middle up and down, pivoting on the held ends, the angle changes until the proper landing is seen and set. One by one, two by two, plank pairs are got out, beveled and installed up to the sheer strake, which is not beveled, unless cutting gains to bring the insides of the planks flush at the ends to ease transom shaping. Using 10 inch boards, four planks per side is about right. With all planks riveted together, it is now time to install transoms.

Patterns must be made for the transoms. This can be done with big enough pieces of cardboard or it can be done with a storyboard and tick stick. If we need to pull the pram's ends together a little to tighten up the joints, this can be done with a strap around the end, or with sticks pushing up from the floor. Then, a stick fastened between the tops of the sheer strakes square to the center line is a great help. Square is set by measuring from the center of the bottom board at one end to the top of the sheer strake at the other end and placing the cross spall stick or strap where the measurements are equal. With cardboard, fitting is likely to be a gradual process of working the pattern stock down close and scribing with a pencil compass for final fit. [Note: In scribing, the compass must be held at the same angle as you sweep it around, vertical and in line with the pattern angle works best usually. If you accurately cut to a properly scribed line the cut piece will fit, moved the compass's span, direction and angle, as though sliding into place.] Both bow and stern transoms should set at flaring angles, not vertical.

Storyboard and tick stick method: With cross spall in place as above, place a flat board, like a scrap of plywood, from cross spall to planks at the desired transom angle. Then with a straight stick with a sharpened point at one edge, slide the stick tight along the storyboard out to the various joints and significant points the transom must meet, making a line on the tick stick edge and a tick on the stick and board, measuring the spans as tick lengths. Different ticks on the stick can be identified as different measurements. The storyboard then holds the pattern of the needed shape in it's system of lines and ticks.

The bow transom will be a single piece but the stern transom will be two pieces, top outside and lapping the lower, the two riveted together. With the pieces fitted, cut crown in the top of the bow transom and the top section of the stern transom. A sculling notch can also be cut in the stern transom top. Fastening with screws, take care to put them in line with the transom so the planks extending past the transoms can be cut and planed flush, and so the fasteners don't come out inside the transom. Now the pram is ready for interior structure, in this case, steam bent ribs, seat risers, seats, quarter knees, and rails.

For steam bent ribs we want air dried, or green, straight grain white oak. Locust, elm, red oak and other hard woods that steam well for bending and have some rot resistance will work, much depends on where you are and what is available. We also need a steam box and a source of steam. The box can be a heavy gauge plastic pipe but I like a simple wooden box long enough to take the longest piece. Cross pieces inside the box, to support wood being steamed, help. There are electric steam generators. I use a propane burner with an iron tank, 1 inch iron pipe nipple on top that fits an 1¼ exhaust hose fed to a matching nipple on the box. I want "cool wet steam", that is, I don't want the box tight enough to produce back pressure and I want the box dripping water from condensing steam.

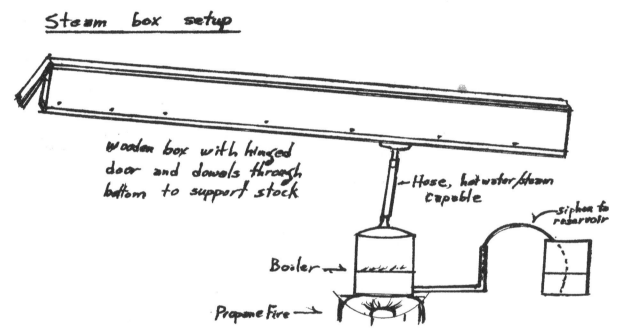

Milling the ribs, I think ½ inch is a little light and ¾ a little heavy, so I'd go with 5/8 inch square. Square section, or close to it, is good because it will twist or bend across the diagonal where more rectangular shaped pieces will only bend on the flat. Floors, in boats, are structural pieces that cross the keel and connect the sides of the hull together at the bottom. In this pram building we bend ribs from gunwale to gunwale, the ribs acting as floors. [If you install sawn frames these will normally be "floor and futtock", floors fastened to bottom board and garboards (and perhaps the first "broad strakes" too) and futtocks carrying on to the rail.] The ends of steamed wood will not bend so we need our rib stock to be longer than the inside span from rail to rail. Extra pieces are also a good idea, first because there is often breakage when bending and the extra pieces can always be bent and held to make knees that will be useful later. When all rib stock is milled and ready, and steam is pouring out of the steam box, start putting some in, not all at once. The "standard" for steaming is one hour per inch of thickness but I find that a little less time is needed with good wood and good steam, and over cooking is a real danger. Put in four or six pieces and later put more in as ribs come out and go into the boat. Have plenty of clamps ready as well as drill and nails for riveting, a hammer also will come in handy. It is good to have the pram lowered to the ground, still on it's strongback, so you can get inside when bending in the ribs.

In 20 – 30 minutes take the first piece out of the steam box, stand back when opening as the steam will pour out HOT. Wearing gloves, reach in for the piece and give it some pre-bend while moving rapidly to the boat (the closer the better as optimal bending time is short). If you can get into the boat your feet will be useful, holding and walking the rib into place. Make sure you are centered for the rib to reach both rails and clamp one end to the sheerstrake, pushing that side to the planks, work across to the other side until you can clamp that side to the sheerstrake too. Then, pushing against the rib where it is not quite tight to a plank lap, rap on the rib end with the hammer to give it a little more bend. When your rib seems as good as it's likely to get, start drilling from the center and pushing nails through the holes as you go, it can help to hold a heavy weight against the rib and drive the nail with a hammer. Drill and nail at the topside plank laps, easily accessible, leaving the sheer for rail construction later and the bottom for when all the ribs are in. Don't rivet until you are done, the nails will hold as they are and there is more rib bending to do. Gets porcupine like inside, but unless you lose your balance you'll be ok. If a stick breaks instead of bending, go on to another unless there's enough left to use elsewhere. If you get all the ribs bent in and still have pieces in the steambox give them good strong, 90 degree, bends or tight U shapes and brace them under a bench or tie the ends with line to hold the bend for later use. Then shut down the steaming operation and get riveting.

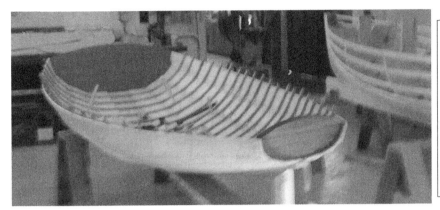

This ribbed out pram will work fine. With pressure from the steamed ribs the sheer line might take a turn that can be planed fair after drawing a fair line with a batten.

    Rivets now going through rib as well as plank lap may need to be bigger than lap rivets, but the process of riveting is the same. Riveting the top of the ribs along the sheer is left until the inwale in riveted in place. Pressure from the ribs will change the shape of the hull, especially the sheer line, if wanted a batten can be clamped along the sheer to establish a sweet line. Plane to the line before installing the inwale. I don't expect all, or even most of the ribs to be tight to the planks at the riveting points. I don't think it matters as long as you don't bend the nail shank in riveting, but it would be fine to cut wedges to fill the spaces, this will call for pulling the nails, drilling through the wedge and replacing the nail before riveting. With all those pointy nails in the boat it is probably safer to rivet starting at the sheer and working down. When all the rivets are set you can cut off the rib ends above the sheer, best to cut square to the plank, which should be a little above level, as inwales are to come and should be flush across the top to the sheer strakes. But, before the inwales come the quarter knees.

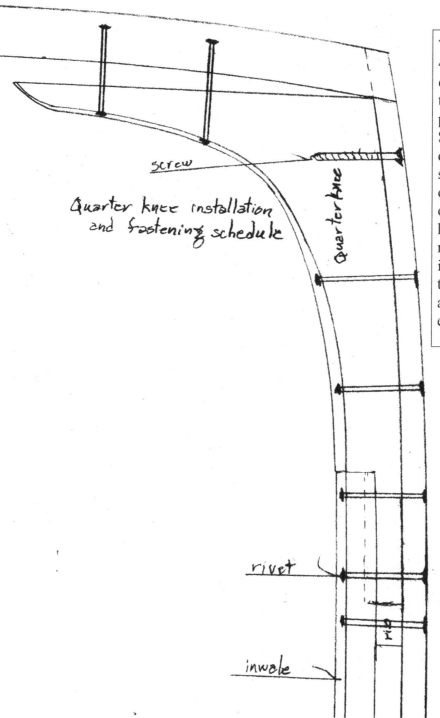

Quarter knee installation and fastening schedule

screw
Quarter knee
rivet
inwale

The pram will have 4 quarter knees, one at each of the transom/sheer positions. For the Spurling rowboat, described subsequently, only one transom means only 2 quarter knees. The knee is rabbeted to take the inwale, completing the structure around the upper edge of the vessel.

Quarter knees tie transoms to sheerstrakes, and are notched to lap the ends of the inwale, tying the boat together on it's upper edge. Ideally, quarter knees are grown knees with the grain sweeping from transom to sheer with a nice fair curve carrying from transom to the notch where the inwale will land, 2 to 3 inches is good for the notch/mortice. In practice grown knees are not always available. Straight grain hardwood like oak can be used but the grain must cross the angle as much as possible, and a piece with some sweep in the grain is better than straight. I have also seen a straight grain piece used as filler in the angle with bent wood around the inside. Again, quarter knees are riveted in place tight to transom and sheerstrake.

Inwales cross the tops of the ribs, ending on the prepared quarter knees where the landing should be the same thickness as the ribs. If fitting an outwale/rubrail, this can be fit and fastened together with the inwale. The inwale might be 5/8 x 1 inch section with the inside corners just slightly chamfered for comfort. The rub should be a little heavier, maybe ¾ x 1 inch and rounded top and bottom. These can be riveted through the tops of the ribs. If you rivet the inwale first, sheerstrake, rib top and inwale, then you could fasten the rub with screws at the ends into the quarter knees and countersunk machine screws/bolts through the sheerstrake under the inwale.

Risers installed against the ribs will support seating, thwarts, stern sheets and bow platform. For seating to be standard 6 inches below the rail, risers will be about 7 inches down. They might well be ¾ x 1 inch, but can be lighter, and get screwed to the ribs. For platforms bow and stern (called bow sheets and stern sheets), install beams across the hull at riser height to support these fore and aft laid seats. It is nice to give the underside of such beams a little shape, curves, ogee, drop point, something other than straight.

It's good to install the thwart, or thwarts, now, then the boat can be taken off it's strongback and a skeg installed before the stern sheets/seat installation complicates fastening. In a 10 to 12 foot pram one thwart is probably enough and leaves leg room for all. Placed about amidship, the single thwart should put the pram a little bow down for rowing alone, which is good, and allow a single passenger to sit in the stern sheets without putting much transom down where it creates drag. 7 to 8 inches is a good width for a thwart. To ensure the thwart is square across the boat, measure from the center at the bow and mark equal distances on both sides. You can notch the thwart ends around ribs but you want the ends to stop short of the planking, it is just as well if the thwart comes to the ribs and is beveled to match the angle of the rib. For looks it is good to put a shallow bevel on the underside of the thwart leaving ½ inch at the edge, beveled back 1½ inches stopping short of where the thwart lands on the riser. Plane a slight chamfer or round on the upper edges for comfort. Run a couple of screws into the riser at each thwart end before installing standing knees – if I haven't said it before, always drill for screws and, for your screw to pull the pieces together tight, drill through the outer piece with a bit the diameter of the screw shank, smaller diameter for the threads below but not smaller than the solid center of the screw (Fuller Machine Co. tapered bits do a pretty good job and come with matching countersinks that work well with bungs cut with their bung cutters).

Thwart relief and riser shape

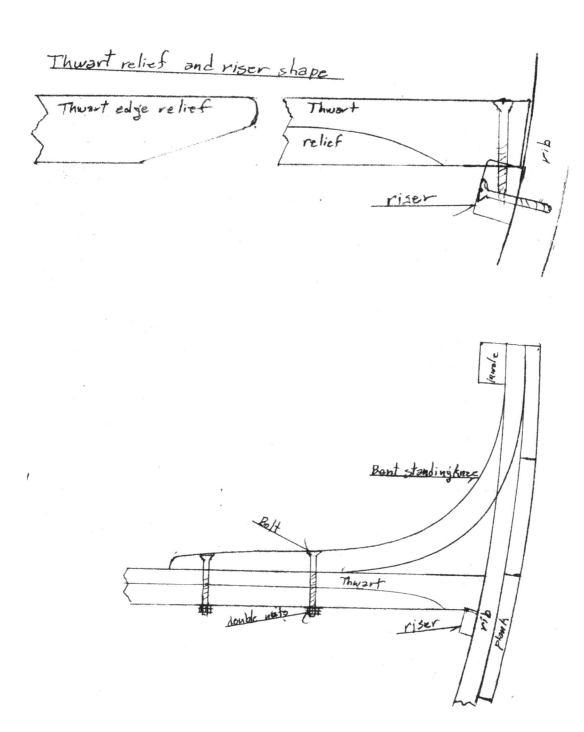

Details of riser, thwart and standing knee construction. Top shows relief of thwart edge. Bent standing knee shown below is fastened to the thwart with flat head machine screws and fastened through inwale from plank with a rivet. If a grown knee, it will be fit to the planks and screw fastened to the planking.

Standing knees on thwarts hold the thwart to it's riser and help resist fore and aft movement when rowing. If you use the thwart as a mast partner for sailing the knees are important for distributing the loads from sail to boat. With grown knees or bent knees I like to have the bottom leg stretch some inches along the thwart. The upper leg of the knee reaches to the rail, behind the inwale, through fastened with a rivet. Here is a place for the spare rib stock bent for later use. These bent pieces will not likely have the exact shape needed but being the molded dimension of the ribs will fit perfectly between inwale and sheerstrake while the lower arm can be planed to lie on the thwart – these bent pieces still have some flexibility especially if you want to relieve some of the bend. The lower leg should be tapered down as it extends along the thwart, for comfort and looks, ending with a little sweep down. Fastenings can be rivets driven up and peened on top or small bronze machine screws with nuts and washers underneath.

With thwarts installed, the pram can be taken off it's strongback but maybe you will want to fit the platform/sheets fore and aft while everything is still stable, fit but don't attach the stern sheets until a skeg is made and fastened to the underside of the bottom board. Cleats fastened to the transoms will support the ends of the platforms/seats. As the hull sides widen away from the transoms, some sort of sunburst or flaring shapes should be used for these constructions. The outside pieces can be extended along the sides of the hull, especially in the stern, but much depends on the stock in hand and what pleases your eye. These pieces will be screwed to the support structure already set in place, but before finishing that job you will want to fit and fasten on a skeg.

The skeg will carry the transom angle aft and reach not quite to the middle of the pram. It should be ¾ inch deep forward, enough to hold a screw from above, and 5 or 6 inches deep aft. If it's bottom edge lines up with the bottom board at it's widest that would be grand though how often will she sit on a flat surface? The skeg needs to be tight to the bottom board, oak or some other hard wood and at least an inch thick would be good.

Spiling for the shape of the bottom, the skeg stock gets cut and planed, square along the curve. Drilling fastening holes through the center of the bottom board will help locate the skeg, then with the skeg held tight to the bottom, drill down from above for screws into the skeg. Bedding the joint between skeg and bottom will help keep water out. When that is all done the stern sheets seat can be finished.

The pram needs oarlocks for rowing, and either metal locks or thole pins need pads on the rails. The oar pivot should be 12 inches from the aft edge of the rowing thwart or 15 inches from thwart middle, said Gerald Smith – a good rule of thumb. Like all rules this is subject to variation as people come in different shapes. I sold one pram to a man who was 6 feet 10 inches tall and had to make a removable thwart to place forward of the rowing thwart so he could comfortably row. Anyway, fit blocking between the sheerstrake and inwale where the pads will be fastened and rivet them in place. The first time I met Gerald Smith, I had just built my first pram. He came up to the pram after I had installed blocky pads on the rails for the oarlocks, quoting his boatbuilding father, Charlton, saying, you can wreck the look of a elegant boat with blocky pads like that when tapering the pad ends or a little ogee will enhance the boats appearance. So, a longer pad with lightened ends is what you want, whether you are installing metal sockets or thole pins. If sockets, mortice the socket and through bolt after drilling and fitting for the oarlock shank. If thole pins, drill about 4 inches apart. I like a tapered pin generally as they are easily replaced wherever you are, if there is any wood about.

Some good oars are about all you need now to put your pram in action. A hole can be drilled in the bow transom to carry a painter, or you could drill through the quarter knees for the same purpose. Now you are ready. For finish I like many coats of raw linseed oil inside and out, this will soak into the wood overnight. Painting the seats and the exterior topsides is a good idea, and if to be kept in salt water, not hauled out between uses, bottom paint keeps marine growth from slowing you down or eating into the bottom.

One of the great things about a pram like this, with it's broad bow reaching out, is the way you can come to a beach or ramp with the bow past the water's edge and walk ashore, reversing the procedure you can walk aboard and when aft you can be floating with your momentum starting you on your way. Best of all though is how well the pram rows. Have fun!

ARTHUR SPURLING ROWBOAT

BUILT AS ANY BOAT CAN BE FROM PLANS WITH OFFSETS

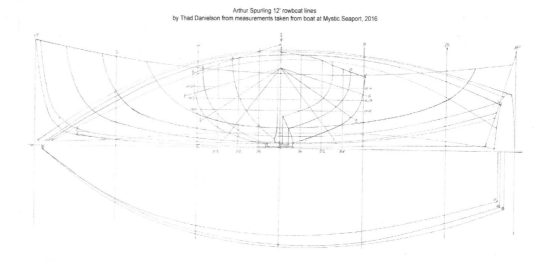

Arthur Spurling 12' rowboat lines
by Thad Danielson from measurements taken from boat at Mystic Seaport, 2016

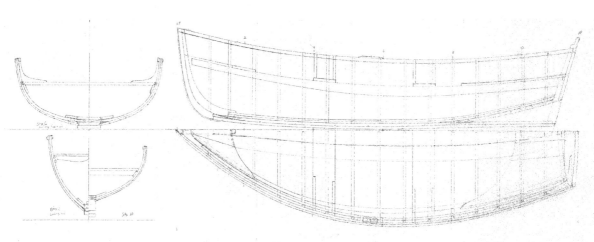

Arthur Spurling 12' rowboat construction drawing
by Thad Danielson based on boat at Mystic Seaport, collection # 1985.79

The pram building described above presented a procedure that leads to different boats, related but different, any time such boats are built. They can be built big or little, and anywhere in between. There are pram designs with a similar look to the one described intended to produce "as planned" boats, one attraction of the pram building procedure is the flexibility in producing boats with different capabilities. There are other types of boats historically, more procedure than plan, that also made such flexibility in capability possible, Whitehalls for one, but the Norwegian pram accomplishes this simply. Now we go on to building to a plan.

I described in the preface how my involvement with the Arthur Spurling rowboat developed. If you want a great rowboat you could hardly do better than this boat, but if you have another boat in mind like a 30 foot sailboat or 26 foot launch the procedure described here will work for you, with additional considerations like decks, rigs and engine installation. Whatever boat you are after building, you will have looked at many options before picking the one you want. Having picked a design and purchased plans, you need to study your plans carefully, thinking about all the details shown and written. In the mean time, you might build the Spurling rowboat, getting comfortable with the building procedure and ending up with a superior tender for the bigger vessel to come.

The Spurling rowboat is a 12' (actually 11'8") open (no deck) rowboat. The lines and construction plan drawings are shown above. If you chose this design you will know it is a carvel planked dinghy of typical shape, but even in the small scale shown here you might pick out some unusual details as well as Arthur Spurling's handling of more common elements. The grown knee stem (and all the other knees, grown hackmatack) was not that unusual in an era when they were common currency amongst boat builders and lumber men, not so common today. The broad plank keel with shoe is unusual. Likewise, the skeg block carrying the planks to the stern post and transom is unusual. When you see the scantling/details list and see that both keel and skeg are cedar, that is unusual. The shoe is oak and the same thickness as the cedar keel. Then, there are no floors, another curiosity. Floors, as mentioned before, are structural connections between the sides of the boat across the keel, usually fastened to the ribs or frames. Arthur Spurling screwed the beveled lower ends of the ribs to the cedar keel, that was it. His were very well regarded boats so we won't argue with success.

iPad photo under floorboards of Spurling rowboat at Mystic Seaport looking along planking to upper keel edge with tapered end of rib on top of keel. Also on top of keel are blobs of rust where steel garboard fasteners have come through the keel. Note how the garboards fly from keel rabbet to rib fastenings toward the upper edge.

In the Preface I spoke about using the iPad camera to see under the floorboards, particularly to see how the garboards and ribs connected to the keel and skeg, as well as what supported the floorboards. One mystery remaining from the pictures involved a series of red lumps on top of the keel where one might expect to see garboard fasteners protruding. These looked to me like rust, where screw tips had gone through the keel and over time had rusted into little rust blobs. This was likely confirmed one day in my class when we had visitors. At the WoodenBoat School, visitors come around almost every day. One day, a couple years ago, a visiting group included a former neighbor of mine. When I told her it was a Spurling rowboat we were building, she said she and her sister had had one forever at their family cottage on Little Cranberry Island, where Arthur Spurling lived and built his boats. Finally she had despaired of maintaining their boat due to iron rot from the steel screws used in it's building. Steel (iron alloy) rusts faster than pure iron, rust is many times bigger than steel and the rusting process produces chemicals that degrade wood (each very destructive), so use silicon bronze screws in boat building if not using copper rivets.

Having studied the plans enough to see how the structure is put together and enough to have questions in need of answers, then there is the details/scantling list to check out, below. There you could start with your questions or go from top to bottom, noting the details for consideration and compiling a materials list. At the top is the hackmatack stem knee. Below that come the cedar keel and oak shoe, both 7/8" thick, then the cedar skeg. The transom material is unspecified but Spurling's was oak though other hard woods would do well. Stern post is oak, as are the steam bent ribs, though unspecified. The planking is cedar. The breasthook is oak. Below that only the hackmatack knees at thwarts and quarters have materials specified because I could not be sure of these parts, but rail pieces and riser would likely be oak, the seats might have been mahogany, but another hardwood or pine a little thicker, would do well. Floorboards should be cedar. The rowlock pads could match the thwarts if hardwood, but they should be hardwood. Ring for painter and half oval should be brass or bronze.

Here is the details/scantling list for the Spurling rowboat with measurements put in feet-inches-eighths format, as measurements are generally given in tables of offsets:

Details/scantlings taken by Thad Danielson from Arthur Spurling rowboat, 1985.79, at Mystic Seaport

Stem	Hackmatack knee sided 0-2-2, molded 0-2-4 at top
	Face and rabbet line of stem: 6" down 0-0-7 and 0-2-2 aft of FP,
	12" down 0-2-0 and 0-3-3 aft of FP,
	18" down 0-3-5+ and 0-5-3+ aft of FP.
	Fore end of keel 12" aft of FP
Keel and shoe	Sided 0-0-7, molded to keel offsets, keel cedar, shoe oak, low point aft 8½" forward of AP.
Skeg block	Cedar, shaped from 4 foot 6" x 8".
Transom	Sided 0-1-0, transom crown 2"
Stern post	Oak, sided 0-1-6 tapered up and down, molded 0-1-0 at top, 0-1-4 at stern sheets, 0-2-4 below transom.
Ribs	Oak, sided 0-1-0-, molded 0-0-5, rounded inside
	Rib spacing +/- 9" starting 10" from stem
Planking	8 each side, cedar, sided 0-0-4, sheer strake bright, planks molded for width as below:

Plank #	ss	1	2	3	4	5	6	garboard
Bow	0-2-0	0-2-3	0-2-1+	0-2-1+	0-2-6	0-2-5+	0-2-7	0-3-0
St 6'	0-4-2	0-4-3	0-3-7	0-3-6	0-3-6	0-4-0+	0-4-2	0-3-1
Stern	0-2-4	0-2-2	0-2-0+	0-2-4	0-2-5	0-3-4	0-3-7	0-4-0

Breast hook	Oak, two piece, sided 0-1-0, 10" legs to first rib, 1/4" crown
Quarter knees	Hackmatack, sided 0-1-0, 9" legs to aft most rib
Inwale	Sided 0-1-0, molded 0-0-5
Riser	Sided 0-0-4, molded 0-1-6 at bow, 0-2-6 amidship and aft, upper edge 7½" below rail
Thwarts	Sided 0-0-6, molded 7¾", thwart tops 6¾" below rail
Standing knee	Hackmatack sided 0-0-7, lower arm +/-9"
Stern sheets	5 planks, sided 0-0-4, points 3' from transom, 17" deep on C/L
Bow sheets	4 planks, sided 0-0-4, points 25" from stem, 17" deep on C/L
Rowlock pads	Sided 0-0-4-, 8½" long with 1 1/16" roman ogee at ends
Floorboards	Sided 0-0-5, three with middle following keel, sides 4" wide aft to middle, tapering to 3" at bow\
Rub rail	Sided 0-1-0-, molded 0-0-4
Painter ring	Inside stem 4" below breasthook
Brass bands	½ inch half oval from breasthook down stem and 4½" along shoe
	Flat plate let into shoe for 5 3/8" and 3" up stern post

Maybe now it's time to put together a material list. Here's an example, the way I think about it.

The hackmatack knee is grand if you happen to have a source or want to go to the expense of ordering one. A spruce knee would be ok too if that is available. Looking at the plan and scantling list you need a knee 2½ inches thick with 2 foot arms, the angle between arms 115 degrees, more or less. Without a grown knee you can construct a stem with 2 or three pieces that are bolted together. At this point what you know is that you want either the grown knee or some oak that will finish at 2½ inches thick (sided 0-2-4), enough to construct a stem.

For keel and shoe, 1 cedar board to finish sided 7/8" and at least 8 inches wide, at least 10' long and 1 oak board with dimensions similar to the cedar.

For skeg, cedar, 6" x 8" x 4'. This may be difficult to find, especially as with any boat timber it must be sawn "clear of heart", that is the center pith of the log should not be in the piece. If not clear of pith the piece will check badly as it dries. It is possible to glue up a block from thinner stock.

For stern post, oak to finish 1¾" x 2½" x 2', could be part of the piece used for the built up stem.

For ribs, oak 30+ pieces 15/16" x 5/8" x 4'. Starting with full 1 inch boards and ripping ¾" strips (to finish 15/16" x 5/8") accounting for 1/8" saw kurf, I would need more than 30 inches of width of 4' boards or 15 inches of 8' boards, remembering that this should be straight grain green or air dry.

The inwales, rub rails and risers can come out of a couple of 12' oak boards and probably leave enough extra material to make up knees and breasthook.

For thwarts and fore and aft seats, there are choices and decisions to make, easily fulfilled taking in consideration what is available. The same can be said for rowlocks and other hardware. With half inch planking on 5/8 ribs, 1 inch #8 silicon bronze wood screws will just work, ¾ inch might be just a little short for good holding without driving them too deep in the plank. With 8 planks a side on 15 ribs, plus stem and transom, with every plank getting two screws at each crossing, that calls for 544 plank fastening screws. With the other parts to fasten I would be inclined to order 700 #8 1" screws. This design also calls for a few longer screws for fastening keel and shoe to the stem, keel and shoe to skeg, and sternpost to transom and skeg – so we will want 100 1½ inch #10s and some 2½ inch #12s. I like slotted screws, thinking about the times someone will want to remove screws later, slots are lots easier to clean out than little pocket types, Philips, square, etc. I know Arthur Spurling used steel screws though he might also have used brass or bronze at other times. Copper rivets are an option if accurate reproduction is not the object. Screws are easy and direct, especially if working alone, but rivets are clamps without splitting forces.

Not mentioned in detail/scantling list are materials needed for making molds and strips needed for ribbanding around the molds when they are set up. A little stock of rough white pine is fine for molds and 16 pine strips 1" x ½" a little over 12' long (for the sheer at least) would be good.

Having had a good look at your plans and thought about materials and construction, it is now time to start lofting, drawing the plans full size and making patterns for parts.

The table of offsets looks like this:

Arthur Spurling 12' rowboat Offset Table by Thad Danielson based on boat in Mystic Seaport Collection	Fore Point (FP) to Aft Point (AP) 11'8", Stations at 2' intervals from FP									
Stations		Stem	2'	4'	6'	8'	10'	Transom		
Height above baseline	sheer	2-3-3	1-11-1+	1-8-4	1-7-4	1-7-3	1-8-5	1-10-5	Transom top	2-1-1
	keel bottom	2-3-3	0-1-5	0-0-4+	0-0-1+	0-0-6+	0-1-1	0-1-3		
	parting line	2-3-1	0-2-5+	0-1-3+	0-1-2	0-2-0	0-5-3	0-8-5		
	Buttock 6"		0-6-1	0-2-3	0-1-5	0-2-3-	0-6-3	0-10-1		
	Buttock 12"		1-2-3	0-4-7	0-3-2	0-4-3	0-8-6	1-0-7+		
	Buttock 18"			0-8-5+	0-5-3	0-7-0	1-1-1-			
Half breadths	Sheer	0-1-1	1-2-0	1-10-3	2-1-5	2-0-3	1-8-1	1-2-7		
	WL 16"		1-0-7	1-10-0+	2-1-1	2-0-0	1-7-5	1-2-2		
	WL 13"		0-11-4+	1-9-0+	2-0-2	1-11-2	1-6-0	1-0-2		
	WL 10"		0-9-6	1-7-0+	1-11-0	1-9-6	1-2-0+	0-6-1		
	Keel	0-0-2	0-1-3	0-3-4	0-4-0	0-3-6	0-2-4	0-0-6		
Diagonals	D A		1-1-6	1-10-5	2-1-5	2-0-5	1-8-1	1-3-1		
	D B		1-2-0	1-10-0+	2-1-0	1-11-7	1-6-6	1-2-5		
	DC		1-2-6	1-8-4-	1-10-4-	1-9-1	1-4-6	1-1-1		
	DA from 1-9-0 above base on CL through intersection of WL16 and Butt 18									
	DB from 1-9-0 above base on CL through intersection of WL10 and Butt 18									
	DC from 1-9-0 above base on CL through intersection of baseline and Butt 18									

Lofting the Spurling rowboat

Lofting starts with a "floor" to draw on. Thin plywood laid down flat is good and, for this 12' boat, two 8' sheets is plenty. I have used paper on a flat floor but paper shrinks and swells with changes in humidity so it's not reliable in changeable conditions. If using plywood it helps to roll on white primer. Using different colored pencils for different elements can avoid confusion but with careful marking as you start, you will quickly know which lines are which.

With a floor prepared, a grid is drawn based on the lines plan and dimensions given in the offset table. As stated in the offset table above, heights in this plan are given "above baseline", in some plans heights are given above and below (+/-) the load waterline (LWL). The lines drawing above developed in producing the plan and is not meant to be reproduced exactly as it appears, for example it would be too wide for a 4' wide floor, with the diagonals drawn below the other views (the 10" waterline can be used as centerline for drawing the diagonals, one of the early elements in the lofting process). Also, we will want the waterlines in the grid drawn out full length.

We start with the baseline, and place the baseline leaving room at what will be the aft end for drawing out the true view of the transom. For the baseline you might use a laser or stretch a string tight over blocks so it stretches free of the floor, whichever method used, carefully mark with a pencil at intervals in the center of the laser line or directly under the string. Then take a good straightedge and draw a line over the marks. Tacking a long batten down along the line will simplify some later operations using "story sticks".

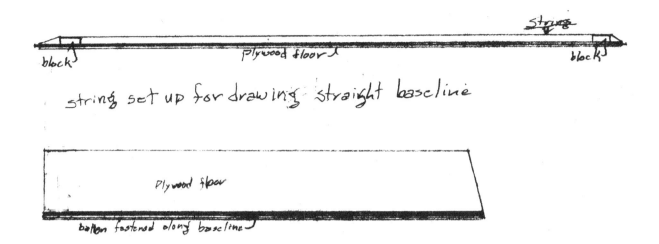

With the base line drawn and, perhaps, solidified, next come the station lines. Starting at the fore point (FP) the station lines are spaced at 2 foot intervals through 10' and then 1'8" to the aft point (AP). Since squares are not always that square, and their use is not always consistent, it is good practice to set up one station like FP using the 3-4-5 rule with 5 being the hypotenuse of a right triangle, then measuring and marking your station intervals from that line at bottom and top to draw the station lines between those points with a good straightedge. Follow a similar procedure for the waterlines, measuring from the baseline. Use the 6' station at the middle for the body plan centerline (CL) and draw the buttock lines parallel to and to each side of the centerline. Mark the point 1'9" up the body plan centerline from which the diagonals radiate and draw the diagonal lines as defined in the offset table. Now the grid is drawn and ready for boat lines.

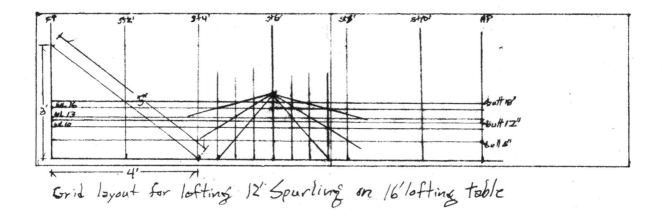

Grid layout for lofting 12' Spurling on 16' lofting table

Drawing boat lines begins with the outlines of the backbone, rabbet and sheer, in both profile and half breadth. Start with the transom line in profile, from height 2-1-1 on AP to the shoe aft, 0-1-3 above base line (that's zero feet, one inch and three eighths, from the offset table) and 8½ inches forward of AP (from the details/scantling list under "keel and shoe"). Now for the sheer profile, mark on the grid the sheer heights at each station from the offset table, noting that the sheer aft ends on the transom line not the AP, then take a fairly stiff batten and bend it through the points marked, as much as possible -- the batten can be held by nails or awls driven into the floor, or by weights. The batten must be sighted along for fair, with adjustments made until the line is pleasing to the eye from end to end, and drawn. This procedure continues for the backbone profile and the rabbet line (where the backbone and planking join, called the rabbet line though there is very little rabbet beyond the stem). A much more flexible batten will be needed for the lower stem, if you use straight grain pine for battens they can be planed down to the point where they will take the needed bend.

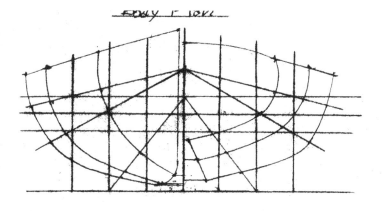

Profile Plan

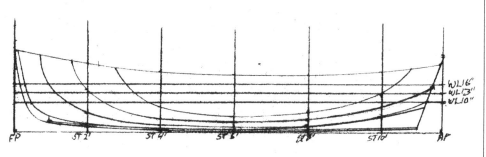

Half-Breadth Plan

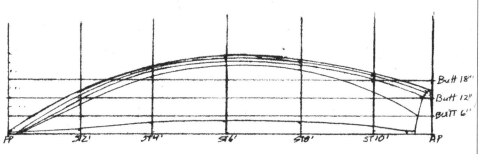

The three plan views to be lofted. Top is the Body Plan, drawn in lofting using the diagonal measurements taken from lofting the Diagonals, generally using a separate Center Line (CL)/Base Line (here I have used the 10" Waterline (WL) as CL for the Diagonals. The sheer and backbone profiles, and the sheer and keel Half-Breadths (HB), are lofted to define the top and bottom ends of the Body Plan lines for each station and transom.

Diagonal Plan

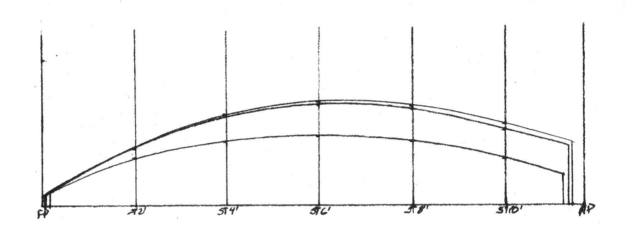

Diagonals lofted on their own CL for station offsets to be transferred to the lofted Body Plan.

With these profiles drawn it is time to put down the half breadths of these same features so they can be transferred to the body plan grid. Now the base line for profile and body plans becomes the center line (CL) of the half breadth plan. This proceeds in the same way, marking offset measurements, connecting marks with battens, fairing and drawing lines. Note that at the transom, the sheer, rabbet and bottom points are squared down from the profile to the half breadth offset, also the rabbet line in half breadth is the same as the bottom except at the stem where the half breadth is half the stem siding, 0-2-2 divided by 2 equals 0-1-1, 1 1/8 inch.

The body plan is drawn with the bow stations on one side of CL/St6 and the stern on the other. Here it is useful to start using "story sticks". These narrow sticks can be set to the base line at the stations and marks ticked off and labeled for half breadths and heights. Using a different stick for each station helps reduce confusion if the sticks are marked for station and ticks are noted for what they mark. The sheer now becomes a series of marks well above the baseline and the backbone a series of marks along CL, spreading away from CL as they approach the baseline. These marks can be connected with lines that will be connected with the body plan shapes for each station but before we can do that we must draw and fair the diagonals.

Looking at the lines drawing, the diagonals cross most hull lines in plan view nearly at right angles. That and the fact that they also follow the lines on which the planks will be running make their fair lines most important for the construction of the boat. So the diagonal lines are drawn out and faired to establish the body plan shapes at each station for the build to be successful. Note that the offset table does not give offsets for the diagonals at FP, but both the distance off CL and distance aft of FP (the planks run to the rabbet line, as will the body plan lines to come).

So we measure along the diagonals to where they cross the stem and from the height of those points get the points aft of FP on the rabbet line. A new CL is needed to draw the diagonals and we might choose waterline 10" (WL10) on the grid, squaring up from WL10 at these points aft of FP the distances measured first. These three points are the fore points of the 3 diagonals, DA, DB, and DC. Placement of the aft end of the diagonals is a little more complicated, but can be judged nearly by seeing where the diagonals cross the body plan transom on the plans. Now, on the station lines enter the offsets shown for each diagonal and draw them out after adjusting them for fair. Again it is a good idea to use a story stick for each diagonal, marking each station offset from CL (in this case WL10 in Profile). These measurements are then carried to the body plan diagonals and marked. Now draw the body plan for each station, using a flexible batten.

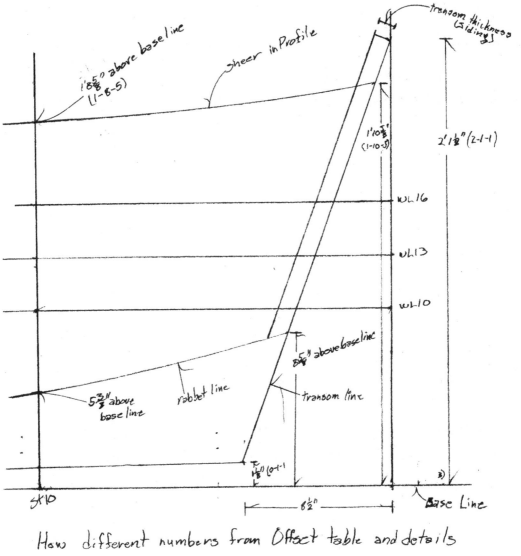

How different numbers from Offset table and details are used in lofting

Aft end of Spurling rowboat lofting, showing how numbers from the offset table are used to develop the Profile drawing. Height (HT) at Aft Point (AP) is (2-1-1), 2 feet 1 1/8 inch, that is the tip of the transom. The bottom of the transom is at the rabbet but the line continues to the aft point of the bottom, given as 1 1/8" (0-1-1) above Base Line and 8 ½" forward of AP. The Sheer at Transom is
1' 10 5/8" (1-10-5) above the Base Line on the Transom line. The inside line is drawn here but is not needed for the original lofting and will be added to later establish the true shape of the transom, inside and out.

With the body plan drawn based on the diagonals, now the waterline in half breadth and buttocks in profile need to be drawn out, partly to check them for fair but mostly to be used in determining the bevels of the stem rabbet and the true shape of the transom inner and outer faces. For these lines, measure off the body plan as it is drawn, don't use the table of offsets. Again, using story sticks is better than measuring with a ruler. Transfer the measurements from the body plan to the other views. For the intersections of the buttocks with the sheer in profile, measure out 6, 12, and 18 inches on the half breadth view, fore and aft, and square from those points to the sheer in profile. Similarly, for waterlines in half breadth, square to the half breadth view from the intersections of the waterlines in profile with the stem and transom. For the half breadth view of the transom, measure the transom half breadths at the waterlines in body plan and mark off the base/center line for these measurements square to the intersection of the appropriate waterlines with the transom line in profile. The transom in half breadth is then drawn connecting these three marks with the sheer half breadth at the transom and the half breadth of the keel/skeg squaring down from the transom base. With all these lines drawn the lofting is now ready for use in drawing out parts and patterning.

Patterning for Spurling rowboat construction

Patterns are needed for the station molds. Patterns are needed for the stem. A pattern is needed for the skeg. Patterns are needed for the inside and outside of the transom. A pattern is needed for the stern post. Length and station half breadths are needed to draw and cut out the keel and shoe. With the stem fastened to the keel, the skeg fastened to the keel and the stern post and transom assembly fastened to the skeg, and the whole backbone fastened to a strongback bracing the stem up to preserve rocker to the forefoot, the station molds will be set up on the keel and skeg so ribbands imaging the planks to come can be fastened around the molds from stem to transom. Ribs will be bent in against the ribbands and then planks will be fastened on as ribbands are removed. Stem, skeg, stern post and transom must be drawn on the lofting for transfer to pattern stock so actual pieces can be cut and shaped that will fit together and, with the keel, be the backbone that will support the rest of the boat.

There are two more lofting jobs still to do, developing the true shape of the transom, inside and out, and establishing the rabbet bevels along the stem, the angles the planks come to the stem.

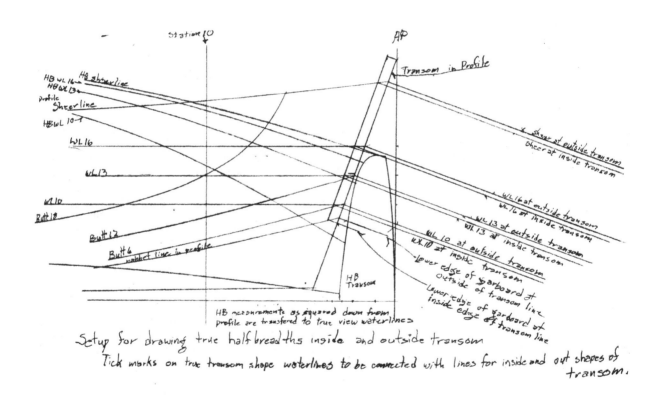

The body plan view of the transom is as looking horizontally with the transom angled away, foreshortened. For patterning, the true shape of the transom is needed, inside and out, so we can cut the bevels for planks that will be coming to the transom at an angle. To do this, start by drawing a line in the profile drawing parallel to and inside the transom line reflecting the transom thickness. Square off at the top of the outside transom line to the inside line because registration is needed between the inside and outside of the transom when it is shaped. Square off these two lines where they cross the waterlines. Now the transom lines on the profile drawing are centerlines for the true views being developed. Here's where having the half breadth and profile drawings drawn on the same grid is useful, a line square to the base line crosses lines on both views at the same point in the boat. A line squared up from the base line to the intersection of inside of transom line and water line 16" also crosses that waterline in the half breadth drawing. Measuring the half breadth of waterline 16" along this line gives the half breadth of that waterline on the true view of the inside of the transom, and is marked on the line squared off the inside of the transom line. This is done for all the new waterlines drawn from the two transom faces. The half breadth of the bottom of the transom is the half breadth of the keel at that point. The sheer half breadth is similarly squared and measured for the inner and outer faces of the transom. Connecting these points with pencil and batten, and drawing a crown curve to the top of the transom, gives the developed true view of the transom to the outside of the planking. To get the actual transom shape the planking thickness as it comes to the transom must be drawn with another set of lines just over 9/16s inside the lines just described, deducting for plank thickness. These lines can now be transferred to pattern stock, and then to transom material.

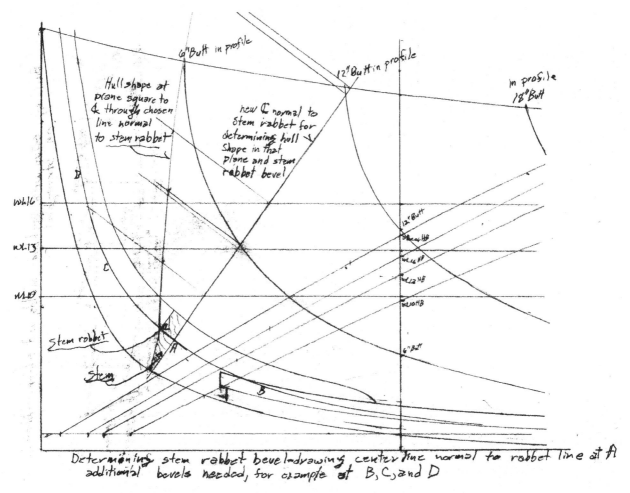

Determining stem rabbet bevel—drawing centerline normal to rabbet line at A additional bevels needed, for example at B, C, and D

The other lofting job is at the other end of the boat, as this is a transom model and not a double ender with stems at both ends, establishing rabbet bevels for the stem. The rabbet line is already drawn and the plank thickness is one half inch, which will be cut square to the faces of the planks as they are brought to the stem. The angles at which the planks come to the stem vary along it's length, so a few points along the stem must be chosen for a good sample with which to work. The procedure is to draw a line square (our old friend "normal") to the rabbet line along the stem. This is a new centerline defining a cross section plane through the half hull. Starting at the stem face the half stem is drawn with the rabbet line point on that cross section. Then, where the centerline drawn crosses waterlines, square off the centerline, defining where the waterline plane passes through this cross sectional plane. Squaring from the baseline through the point where new centerline and waterline cross to the waterline half breadth line, measure and mark that distance on the newly drawn waterline. Where the new centerline crosses a buttock line, square off the new centerline and mark the distance off CL of that buttock, 6" for the 6" buttock. At least a couple of hull points is good as the planking shape coming into the stem is likely to be a curve, but when you connect these points to the rabbet point on the stem cross section this will be the cross sectional shape of the hull defined. With that line coming to the rabbet square into the stem half breadth ½ inch for plank thickness and draw a line parallel to the plank line for the inside of the plank, where this line crosses the outside half breadth of the stem cross section will be the bearding line or inside point of the rabbet at that cross section. The points established should all be drawn and carried through to the keel where it joins the stem. At the sheer the bevel is already pretty well given in the half breadth drawing. Along the keel and skeg to the transom the bevel is given by the station molds and transom quite accurately enough.

The true shapes of the transom faces are established and the bevels at the stem, but the actual stem shape has to be drawn in profile before patterning. If using a grown knee as Spurling did then it will be drawn as a single piece. The notch at the bottom to catch the bow end of the keel, with the stub against which the shoe lands, has to be drawn as well as the arm reaching over the keel, to which the keel is fastened in setting up the backbone. The profiles of keel, shoe and skeg are drawn as well as the stern post. For the skeg we have the rabbet line, but must have 7/8" above that line for landing and shallow rabbet reflecting the shallow angle the garboard takes.

If there is no adequate grown knee then a jointed stem is laid out making use of available materials. This was the case in one WoodenBoat School class where we laid out a three part stem, upper arm (stem), lower arm (forefoot), and joining knee (gripe). This worked out very well in white oak with all pieces bolted together.

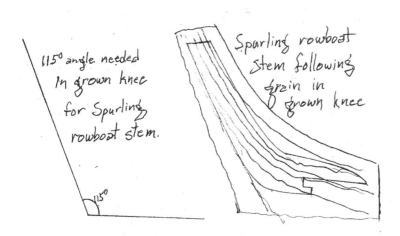

The lofted stem suggests a 115 degree grown knee would be ideal. Slight variation on that shape can work, but that is what to order if you have a source for grown knees. In laying the stem pattern on the knee, make sure the sweep of grain carries through the curve.

Stem layout and stem as made with holes drilled for stopwaters. Note, stopwaters are set between bolts.

Whatever we have for stem it is important to consider placement of stopwaters, starting when drawing the shapes and rabbets for patterning. Water is H2O, two very small hydrogen atoms and one medium sized oxygen atom, making it a very small molecule. Water goes through the smallest crack and where there are joints in the backbone water will follow the joint if it can, between the caulked joints on the outside of the hull. To stop this leakage a hole is drilled from rabbet to rabbet through the joint and a softwood plug or dowel, pine preferably, is driven through and trimmed off flush with the rabbet so that when the planks are caulked the caulking runs across the end of the stopwater.

The body plan is drawn to the outside of the planking. Because the planking called for is ½ inch finished, the outside line of the molds must be ½ inch or a little more inside the lofted lines of the stations. Why "a little more"? The stations are square to the center line and base. Amidship, planks land square to the mold and a half inch reduction will work perfectly, but toward the ends, especially the stern, where planks come to the mold maybe fifteen degrees off square, take off another sixteenth or a little more, that for station 10' and the transom too. For the station molds make marks ½ inch inside the body plan line (9/16 for station 10') and draw lines through the marks with a flexible batten.

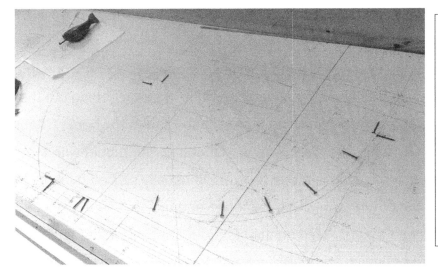

Setup for transferring shape from lofting to plywood for Spurling rowboat Station 8 pattern. Nail heads are driven into the lofting material. Pattern plywood will be placed on top of nails and pressed down to mark pattern lines that will be drawn to battens. Center line and sheer lines are important.

How can shapes be transferred from the lofting floor to pattern stock like thin luan plywood? If lofting is on plywood, one way is to take drywall nails, steel ring shank nails with sharp flat heads, and lay them flat with the head on the lines, drive the head into the top plywood laminations so they will stay in place. For the half breadth station molds and transom don't forget to include marks for the CL and sheer. Then place pattern stock carefully on top of the nail heads and apply pressure, even rapping with a hammer. Lifted, dents from the nail heads should be visible and identifiable. Batten, draw lines and cut out the pattern. If you have lofted on paper or mylar, lines can be transferred by punching holes with awl point or nail. When patterns are cut out and successfully checked with the lofted drawing, then fashioning molds and backbone pieces begins. Be sure the rabbet lines are transferred to the stem pattern(s), then small holes drilled along the lines make transferring the rabbet, apex and bearding lines possible to both sides of the stem for cutting matching rabbets.

Building the Arthur Spurling Rowboat

Is everything ready now?

At the WoodenBoat School, every year there has been a group of 3 or 4 working on lofting when we get to making patterns and they have gone on to work on getting out the parts. Others are working on the pram and finishing a previously started rowboat. People jump back and forth, for example, when the stem is ready for cutting the rabbet with the three lines drawn on both sides, the cutting is a one person job usually started by the person who got the stem out, but others want the experience and by the time the rabbet is done three, four or more have had a turn. "Getting the stem out" involves either finding a grown knee that fits the pattern or finding some 2½ inch oak for making up the stem.

Jointing to start thicknessing (siding) for a straight stem. Tracing with the pattern, cutting with the bandsaw, shaving with planes and chisels, until the stem is shaped and gets rabbeted.

The three lines defining the rabbet are the rabbet line on the outside, the apex line marking the deepest point in the rabbet, and the bearding line on the inside. It can be helpful to set a circular saw at the shallowest depth along the apex line and saw along that line, again all motion must be forward as any backward movement with the blade spinning will cause the back of the blade to pull the saw back out of control. With the saw cut made, chisel and mallet are called for to connect the lines. Remember, the distance between the rabbet and bearding lines is the hypotenuse of a right triangle with the apex at the right angle, the distance between the rabbet line and apex being plank siding (thickness). With the rabbet shape chiseled out at stages along the stem, the wood between can be chiseled out with attention to grain, until the finished rabbet can be cleaned up with rabbet plane and chisel paring (the latter especially at the outside of the sharp forefoot turn).

[Grown knees seldom come in the desired thickness and present one particular difficulty in resawing that needs to be kept in mind. This cutting is usually done on the bandsaw. The bandsaw blade moves toward the table with it's hooked teeth pulling whatever is being cut down onto the table with force. Resawing a grown knee, cutting along the leading arm goes as any straight cut but then comes the bend and the knee must be pivoted so that the coming arm will be tight to the table. If this pivot is not done with care, the blade will take control. This applies to cutting a big grown knee for a stem or small ones.]

Similarly, for the transom, the lumber pile is searched through. Using an 18" board, if one is in the pile, is not the best option, because wood cups as humidity changes it's better to use narrower boards. Arthur Spurling used oak, at the WB School we have used iroko because it's there and for a fancier look. The students usually argue for gluing up a blank and I tell them to spline, using pine for the spline, the stern post fastenings will hold the transom together. The spline should be a press fit. The groove can be cut on the table saw or routed out, the pine spline cut and fit, a centerline marked on each side and the inner and outer transom patterns aligned, traced, and traced, flipped. Then cutting and planing bring the transom to final shape.

The stern post is oak, sided 1 7/8 inches, molded 2½ inches. With a blank of the dimension as long as the pattern, almost 2 feet long, the pattern can be applied, traced and the lines cut to. A bandsaw with sharp blade and good 90 degree setting is a real help here but the cuts can be made by handsaw too, with care, cleaned up with plane and chisel. The profile cut, draw the tapers and plane to the lines.

The keel doesn't get a pattern. For the keel, bend a batten on the profile view lofting, along the keel as drawn, marking the batten for the length and station locations, then measure the half breadths at the keel ends and stations. With the keel length and width in mind, go to the cedar pile and find a good looking piece for the job. With a choice in hand, planed to the desired 7/8 siding (thickness), draw a centerline and use the marked batten to locate and mark the ends and stations on the cedar. Square from the centerline at these marks where the half breadths get measured out and marked so a batten can be used to draw the finished shape of the keel. Cut, again slightly wide of the lines, and plane to finish.

The skeg block remains to be shaped, another job for a sharp bandsaw blade and square table, though other means will work. The aft section of keel is flat, without rocker, so shaping starts with jointing on an 8" face. We should have a pattern for the skeg profile to apply to the block to trace the shape as developed from the lofting. Cutting that out we can use the pattern to locate the skeg half breadths for drawing a centerline and outline on the top of the now tapered block. Cut outside those lines and plane the skeg into shape.

With all the backbone pieces finished (as far as possible) it makes sense now to stick them together, sort of, so the rabbets can be cut in the keel and skeg. Holding the stern post in position on the end of the keel, the skeg can be placed on keel and against stern post. The notch in the sternpost for the transom marks the inside edge and angle of the garboard, this line carries across the sternpost and down the skeg to the keel. On the skeg this line (the bearding line) should be between 3/8ths inch and ½ inch below the top edge of the skeg. Where this line comes to the keel it sweeps in a fair curve, not too tight, to run slightly above the middle of the keel so the rabbet line will be at the bottom of the keel through the middle of the boat. This happens on both sides of these pieces. A similar process takes place forward with the stem and keel. When these lines are drawn the rabbets are best cut now, before assembling the backbone. On the stern post the rabbet can be started with a shallow cut at the bearding line with a saw, the rabbet then finished with chisel or rabbet plane. For the cedar keel and skeg, a utility knife cuts along the bearding line easily and with the same knife cutting back into that cut leaves a vee to work as a guide to the paring chisel or rabbet plane for finishing the rabbet. The bevels for these rabbets come from the station molds and transom, and are quite consistent aft of station 2. Where there is change of bevel along a rabbet it is important to cut a rolling bevel without any quick changes in angle that would create a hard spot.

Before putting the backbone together it probably makes sense to make molds for the stations. 8" to 12" white pine boards serve nicely for this, with matching pieces cut out to the patterns already to hand. Marking the sheer is important, and the centerline at bottom and top of mold. Measuring the desired span between sheer points on the mold and holding the centerline tight at the bottom, fasten cleats across the bottom and top of the mold with CL marked, preferably keeping the cleats all on one side.

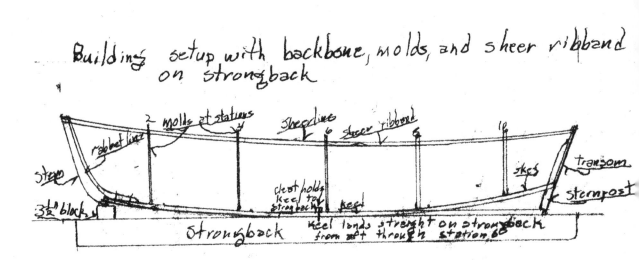

Building setup with backbone, molds, and sheer ribband on strongback

Now! everything is ready for actual building, but where to start? The easiest place to start is fastening the stern post to the transom. Making sure the transom is seated tight in the stern post socket, the transom centerlines, top and bottom, line up and the post is centered on the transom centerline, clamp this construction together. Fastening should be fairly hefty screws, maybe #12 1½ for the top screws as the total thickness is just over 2 inches and in order to bung over the screw head, we countersink a good 3/8 inch when drilling for the screws. At least 2 screws in the top transom section are needed. For the lower section of transom, where the stern post is thicker, longer screws might be used. As always, it is good practice to stagger fastenings so they aren't all run into the same grain line and space the screws evenly.

Laying the keel on it's side, or standing it up for fastening to the stem, might come next. Again, the centerlines are used to position the pieces. Whenever two pieces are being screwed together the pilot hole carrying the shank of the screw should be the same size as the screw shank, then as the threads pull the screw into the far piece the joint will be pulled tight, even when going through cedar into oak. The pilot hole into oak or hackmatack needs to be a little deeper than the screw will go and smaller than the outside thread diameter but bigger than the screw's solid interior, screws will break if driving is too hard. Screw placement needs to be on both sides of stopwater placement, fore and aft. There should be at least 3 inches of keel ahead of the point where the stopwater will be set crossing the keel/stem seam with outside edge near the outside edge of the rabbet, where the keel/garboard seam will be caulked. (This is a caulked carvel hull with the seam along the backbone and all the plank seams caulked, which must be allowed for in getting out planks.)

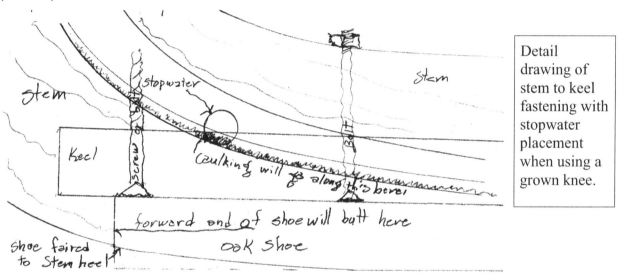

Detail drawing of stem to keel fastening with stopwater placement when using a grown knee.

The skeg gets fastened to the keel, but it might be easier to fasten the sternpost/transom assembly to the skeg first, easier because they have flush faces at the bottom and, with them connected, the keel can be positioned easily as it comes hard against the base of the stern post. Fastening the skeg to the stern post is best done with screws as long as you can get your hands on, because they will be going into cedar endgrain (not the best for holding fasteners). Again, drill the sternpost with a bit the diameter of your screw shank, staggering the fasteners, and countersink for bunging. Now the stem/keel assembly can be fastened to the stern assembly. With all in position on the bench, a couple of short screws, skeg into keel, toward the forward end of the skeg will hold the parts together, then (again, aware a stopwater will be placed through the rabbet between the keel and skeg) screws will be run from below from the keel into the skeg. With the wide keel and skeg, locate the screws in pairs not too close to the edge, maybe 1½ to 1 inch going aft every 9 inches or so, with a final screw into the stern post.

With the backbone all fastened together it is time to fasten it to the strongback and fasten the building molds at the stations. Aft of station 6' the keel is straight and will lie flat on a plank strongback but the heel of the stem must be lifted up 3½ inches by measurement from lofting, by placing a block there on the strongback. A cleat must be used either just forward or aft of station 6' to hold the keel down to the straight strongback at that point – space must be left for station 6' mold and the ribs to come. My plan drawing shows ribs just forward of station 6' so better aft of the station. Your rib layout may be different, don't worry about that but make allowance for all these parts.

Now is a good time to drill and install stopwaters. If the stem is not a grown knee but built up, then stopwaters through the stem joints might well have been drilled for, stopwaters driven and trimmed, after the rabbet was cut, but now that the backbone is all fastened together and secure, the rest can be installed. I drill with a brace and a ½" bit, with the bit's lead screw in the joint, keeping the point in the joint. Direction to the other side is helped by drawing a line between the desired points but holding a finger on the other side and aiming for it is useful too, we tend to know where that finger tip is. With holes drilled, pine dowels can be carved out to drive through the hole, then cut with saw and trim with a sharp chisel. Dowels are most accurately made with a dowel plate which can be made by drilling through heavy steel or iron with a bit of the desired thickness. With wood shaved down to near that thickness it can be driven through the plate, the burr on the edge of the hole shaving the dowel to size.

With the backbone all set up on the strongback, hopefully supported at a good working height, now the station molds are fastened to the keel. Toe nailing with screws seems to work fine. The center mold can be centered on the station line but must be square to the center line. Forward molds have their forward faces on the station lines, aft molds have their aft faces on the station lines, this so when ribbands bend around the molds they will be touching the molds on station. Plumb and square can be determined by measuring from the stem, now, but needs to be checked as ribbands are fastened in place.

Ribband spacing wants marking before fastening. I took the measurements of plank widths from the Spurling rowboat, fore, aft and midship, so 7 marks to make on the stem, station 6' and transom, and 8 ribbands to apply, starting at the sheer, with the top of the ribbands crossing the marks. 1" x ½" ribbands should bend fair around the molds and get fastened without distortion, if they don't it's time to go back to the lofting and pattern making process and see what happened, and time to make a decision on what to do -- live with it, make an adjustment or remake a mold. Starting with the sheer ribband, each mold can be plumbed and squared, as fastening proceeds, then the rest of the ribbands can be bent around the marks and fastened. If the sheer ribband looks slightly out of fair, now is the time to give the sheer the sweet line everyone wants to see. Suddenly it looks like a boat, a leaky boat but very much a boat, all it needs now is planking but first ribs need to be bent in, screwed to the keel and tied to the ribbands.

Ribbands are literally bands around the molds to which steamed ribs are bent, securing the ribs prior to planking, they also mark the upper edge of the planks. For the Spurling rowboat we use Arthur Spurling's plank schedule but few plans come with that detail. The object in ribband spacing is aesthetic and practical, having good looking plank lines and making planking possible, with the hull shape and plank stock at hand. This can be done by eye, but it can help to make decisions using the widest mold, deciding how planks should cross that mold and changing plank widths proportionally with the change in span on the other molds running to stem and stern. Arthur Spurling's plank layout works very well, but nothing is cast in stone until planks are hung and if planking doesn't fit the initial plan as they are hung from garboard up, the plan can be adjusted along the way, though the topside planks are what will be most seen, we want them looking right. Spacings from one side are carried over to the other side so both are done the same way.

Spurling rowboat with ribbands, ribs bent in, upside down ready for planking

Again, with ribbands fastened in place, it's time to have the rib stock ripped out and milled to desired dimensions. Our plan calls for rounding inside rib edges, which can be done with a router or router table, or plane. For pram building, as described above, the ribs were run from rail to rail, this is not unusual for many small boats. In many plans ribs come to the keel or are pocketed into the keel. Most boat plans call for floors crossing the keel, often fastened to the ribs on either side, connecting the hull sides together. Arthur Spurling cut away the underside of his ribs on a bevel 2 to 4 inches long and screwed them to the keel top, with the outside edge coming to the edge of the keel. This can be seen in the cross sectional views on the construction drawing. At the bow the bevel is cut on top so the rib can be screwed to the side of the stem and fair into the rabbet. The first three ribs in the bow will be different from the rest and need to be marked or otherwise identified when taken from the steambox. It's a good idea to drill the rib end for screwing before steaming, one less step later.

With the steambox dripping, steam pouring out, start putting in ribs. Stand back whenever opening the box as hot steam will pour out, after the initial blast of steam, things are much more benign. With our 5/8ths thick ribs I'd start pulling pieces out in a half hour or a little less, if the first piece seems too stiff a little longer might do it, but there might be cool air leaks to stop or it might be difficult wood – then again, it might be stiff but bend fine anyway. If a piece breaks, toss it and get another. It's always good to have extra stock milled and ready when bending. Gloves help, pulling hot wood out of the box and pre-bending as you move to the boat.

We can all use a little help but it is possible to bend in the ribs alone, it just takes planning. Using short sheet rock or self tapping screws for screwing to the keel or stem would be quick and easily replaced after the rib is secured to the ribbands, even cool after steaming is finished. With the lower end secured, a few clamps, pushing and a hammer rap on the top of the rib to push the bend out tight to the ribbands work, along with over bending by hand and rolling the bend into place. Clamps get in the way (and few of us have more than 200 spare clamps lying around), so plastic wire ties can be used to secure the rib/ribband joints but wire rebar ties twisted tight also do a good job. Building a big boat, screws into the rib might seem the thing to do. With the bottom end fastened, tighten to the ribbands from the bottom and move up. When steaming is all done, ribs secured, cut the long ends off but not quite down to the sheer, yet. Next comes planking.

Planking and fairing is a lot easier upside down. A little extension on the 2' and 10' molds, like bits of 2x8 fastened across the tops of the molds, will support the set up on a couple of saw horses, the ones that have been supporting the strongback will do nicely. Again a little help from your friends would make this move easier but even with the strongback connected (it's needed to maintain the keel shape) the whole package is not too heavy. The "boat", upside down now, awaits spiling and planking.

Three planks to go on this side after this one gets fastened. That sheer batten looks mighty unfair toward the stern but the planking will come out fine in the end.

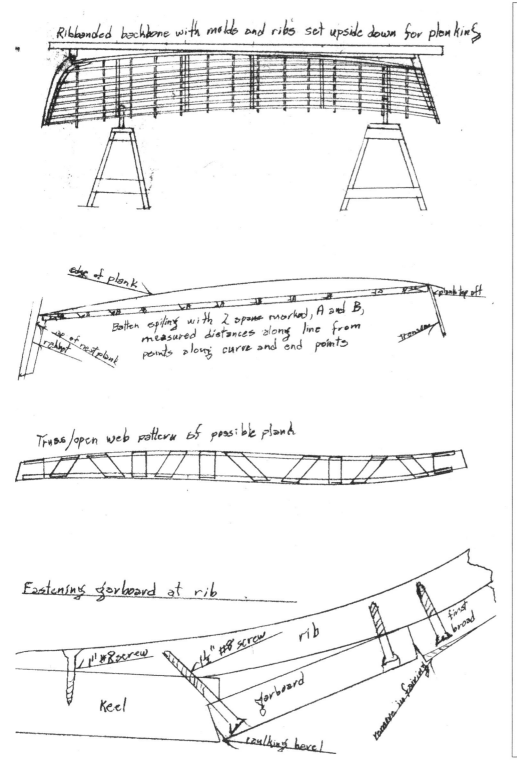

Spurling rowboat framework in ribbands upside down on saw horses ready for planking.

Batten bent around ribs without edgeset, ready for spiling using one method or another, compass or tick stick. Even using the compass, a tick stick is good for locating stem rabbet shape of the plank hood end.

Truss spiled pattern of actual plank shape. Combining diagonal and square spacers ensures that the shape is accurately captured.

Fastening of rib to keel and garboard to keel and rib. Fasten through keel into rib at each rib, into keel between ribs.

Spiling gives the shape of the plank to come. My spiling methods are a spiling batten or a truss construction. The garboard butts to the rabbet and it's upper edge comes to the points marked by the top of the lowest ribband on the upturned mold, so, before spiling, the ribband on one side needs to be taken off after drawing lines on the ribs along it's upper edge. After spiling and marking the line on plank stock, the width of the plank is measured at each rib where the upper edge was marked before removing the ribband.

Batten spiling involves taking a strip of wood as long as the boat, and at least 2 inches wide, and clamping it to the ribs between the rabbet and the marks for the plank top. The batten can be trimmed to follow the rabbet up the stem or it can stop close to the stem, but it must bend and twist to land on the ribs between the desired plank edges without being forced. Forcing the batten sideways to stay within a desired area is called edge set. With the batten in position, landing with the same range of bend and twist as the plank will have, a pencil compass can be used to make arcs on the batten with the point held at staggered positions along the installed plank edge, as long as the compass setting is recorded for each spot. With the batten placed on plank stock the compass procedure is reversed with the point held at two points on each batten arc, scribing crossing arcs on the plank stock, the crossing point defining the corresponding point on the plank. I have come to like using a tick stick to the same end. I have used a short ruler with good results, scribing along the ruler edge and ticking the line at a measured number, doing this along the plank edge and into the stem rabbet. With all the points marked, a batten is bent to the points and the plank outline drawn.

Truss or open web spiling is the construction of a pattern that will hold the shape of the plank. For this method two light and flexible strips are stapled or otherwise held along the edges top and bottom of the plank to come, these strips are connected normally and diagonally along their lengths (staples work but a hot glue gun works well too) creating a beam that holds the plank shape. This structure is then placed on the plank stock and traced around so the plank can be cut out.

I cut the plank out with a circular saw, outside the lines, and then plane to the lines. For cutting I want a firm level support, like a good stiff plank supported at elbow height. Sticks laid across the stiff plank support the plank stock and keep the saw from cutting what might be the planking bench. I've often used clamps to hold a plank vertical for planing but a real planking bench will have one vice or more to do the job. If using thick stock for planking and resawing, then I take special care to have the planed edge square across so the two planks will be the same. If tracing the second plank from the first, the time for that is when done planing to the traced lines on the first plank.

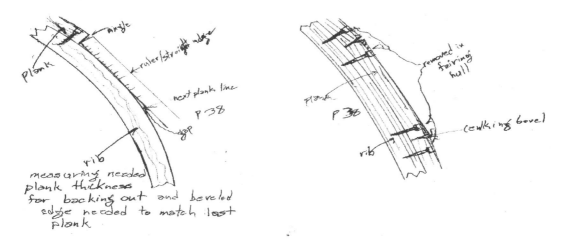

Next comes planing to thickness. For carvel planking the inside of the planks are shaped to land on the rib. The Spurling rowboat garboard has a little reverse curve on it's outside. The inside flies between the rib and the rabbet. A convex shape on the inside edge will land the plank on the rib where it is fastened and a little backing out along much of the plank will allow the plank to fair nicely with the planks to come, round sided above the garboard. To have a ½ inch plank, the garboards needs to be planed to c. 9/16ths so when they are coved out 1/16 inch the final thickness will be as specified. Cut the concave shape on the inside after thicknessing, then start fitting the planks to the hull. With all the planks, shape changes throughout the length of the boat. With the garboards, convex inside shape ends short of the stem, pay attention to the changing shape of the hull.

When I say "fit the plank" I mean to clamp it in place, with the inside shaped properly, checking how well it fits to the rabbet or the adjacent plank, marking the plank where changes are needed to make it fit tight, then taking it to the bench to plane to the marks. When making these changes you will note that if you plane a little off one end of a plank the other end will move away, so these adjustments must be made with the fit of the whole plank in mind. A sharp block plane is the tool of choice here. When the plank is ready to fasten in place, a little edge setting to tighten the joint is a good idea. There are edge setting clamps, clamping to a rib with a screw that will push the plank tight but this can also be done with a clamped block and wedges.

As planking progresses up the hull every plank will be backed out on the inside face but the center of the cove is seldom in the center of the plank. Place a straight edge (I usually use a 6 inch combination square) on each rib with one end on the lower plank and rock the straight edge until the space between rib and rule is the same at each edge of the plank to come. That space will be the amount over ½ inch the plank needs to be, to start, and where the rule is touching the rib will be the deepest point of the cove. For the Spurling rowboat the depth of backing out varies between $1/16^{th}$ and $3/32^{nd}$ inch. The other thing to notice when doing this is the angle between the edge of the lower plank and the end of the ruler. Ideally the plank will be fit so that the plank seam is tight, inside and out, then a caulking bevel will be cut on the outer edge of the coming plank. The caulking bevel should be about $1/3^{rd}$ of the plank thickness and $1/16^{th}$ inch off the outside, $1/16^{th}$ being plenty of space to roll in a thread of cotton wicking, for caulking. Be aware also that as planking proceeds, the planks backed out, the plank edges are more than ½ inch away from the ribs at angles that will be planed off later when fairing the hull. This affects the caulking bevel but also means fasteners are driven for the heads to be at least 1/16th inch below the surface.

It strikes me, writing this, how much the builder has to have the whole building process in mind from the start. Here we are just about to fasten on the first planks and have to consider fairing and caulking that won't happen until planking and all interior structures are installed, just before painting. This is why plans need to be studied and restudied – which makes me think of a story told by a friend of mine.

My friend's father bought a new built but unfinished Friendship Sloop hull. He had it brought it to Basel Day, rolled out the plans and talked to Mr. Day about how he wanted the boat finished just as shown in the plans. Yes, that was fine. As he was leaving, Basel Day rolled up the plans and slid them into a cubby hole over his desk. Months later, word came that the boat was finished and ready for launching. When all this business was concluded, everything just as specified, the owner remembered to ask the builder for the plans. Going to the cubby hole over the desk the builder pulled them out, dusted them off and handed them over. Basel Day knew the plan and hadn't needed the plans at all. It does help to have that kind of command of the plan and the process of producing the boat. That's why I say to study the plans until confident that all the details are clear, there will still be questions but being able to think in terms of the whole structure will make all the difference.

Planking over 5/8th inch is usually bunged, meaning a countersink at least ¼ inch deep after fairing. With planking under 5/8th that would leave barely half of the plank thickness under the fastener head, or less, greatly reducing the strength of the fastener's holding power. Another fastening detail is the position of fasteners. First, not too close to the edge, ½ inch is good, and, second, as in other fastening, stagger fastenings into the oak. The ribs sided 15/16 inch, the screws on adjoining planks should not be in the same line so just a little jog from side to side when drilling for fasteners.

I've had arguments with people about the terms "sided" and "molded". The sense I make of these terms is that "sided" refers to thicknessing, the thickness of the stock that comes to the bench, or shop, to be further shaped, milled or otherwise "molded" by the boat builder. In the case of our ribs "sided 15/16, molded 5/8", I see one inch oak boards (coming from the saw mill at 1 1/8 or, better, 1¼) planed for thickness to 15/16, ripped to ¾ strips, planed to 5/8, rounded with the router on one side with a 3/8 rounding bit, bevels cut on one end for fastening to the backbone, and finally steamed and bent to the ribbands. The stem stock was planed to the 2 ¼ inch sided dimension before being finished to the lofted stem molding.

With the first garboard plank ready for fastening it is time to fire up the steambox again. The twist taken between midship and stem is likely too much for any but the most flexible plank, so it's the better part of valor to steam the garboards. Only the forward ends need steaming. Typically the steambox door at one end has a slot cut in it so the end of a plank can be slid in with rags stuffed around to close the opening (fill the slot with rags when not in use or have a different door). Cedar and other softwoods require less steaming than hardwoods like oak, so the ½ inch plank should be pliable in 15 minutes. Not a bad plan to steam the second set of planks too, better safe than sorry, as planking moves up the hull there is much less twist required so splitting is not likely.

Steamed, garboards are first clamped in place, lower edge in the rabbet and upper edge on the ribs, caulking bevel showing along the keel and stem rabbet. If the fit isn't tight enough or the caulking bevel too tight, wait until the plank cools, then mark where adjustment is needed, remove and trim to fit better – the plank will straighten out some but should go back without trouble. A very important detail with carvel planking is to make sure the plank seam is tighter at the inside than the outside, so pressure on the caulking will tighten the seal instead of opening the seam. With the plank clamped and looking good, drill and fasten. Because the Spurling rowboat has such a shallow keel/skeg rabbet, fasteners there must be driven at an angle, fasteners into the transom need careful drilling too, not to come through inside and with heads inside the outside transom plane, the rest of the fasteners are driven normally. Along the rabbet, fasteners should be every 3 inches including into the ribs above keel and skeg.

One by one the ribbands are removed after marking along the upper edge, spilings made, and planking stock picked through for the ones best for the planks at hand. For each set of planks the depth of backing out is measured before thicknessing. Run through the planer for thickness, centers and depths for backing out are marked on the plank blanks, and backing out planes cove out the planks until a final sanding smooths any ridges. A random orbit sander with round pad, held at an angle so the working edge matches the cove will do a good job of smoothing the cove. The edge and bevel fit of each plank must be checked and adjusted with a block plane before cutting the caulking bevel on the lower outside edge to be ready for final clamping and fastening. One by one, until the last ribbands are off and all planks in place. The planks should overhang the transom when installed. Once each plank is fastened this can be sawn off flush with the transom face.

All the planking might have been done with the hull upside down or the set up might have been turned upright for the topside planks, but with planking done it's time to be upright again to remove the molds and install interior structure. After the last ribbands were removed, only the screws toe nailed into the keel hold the molds in place, but cross spalls are needed to keep the hull shape after the molds are gone. These will be narrow boards placed across from sheer to sheer with cleats on the underside tight against the sheer strake. Two cross spalls will do, near the 4' and 8' molds. The cleats can be lightly screwed to the sheer or the tops of ribs. Then the molds come out.

With the molds out of the way, the boat's interior lies open to view except for the cross spalls. To install the inwale, the cross spalls might need to be removed, but the breast hook, quarter knees, seat risers and thwarts can be fitted and installed, at which point the cross spalls can be removed for good. The inwales join to the breast hook and quarter knees which come first in any case. Gerald Smith's rule for rowing thwarts and row locks was thwarts should be 6" below rail height, and row locks 12" aft of the aft edge of the thwart or 15" aft of thwart center. Arthur Spurling placed the thwarts lower, 6¾ inches down. Take your pick. Spurling's thwarts were sided ¾, for which he would have measured down 7½ inches and marked on the ribs where the top edge of the riser will land.

My old friend Bill Hawkes said, "Thwart is pronounced thought, in Marblehead", just as quay is pronounced key and buoy boy. It's good to keep up these practices, like building wooden boats. Risers in rowboats support the thwarts and sheets, but also act like bilge stringers in larger craft, supporting the hull structure, tying the rib structure together on the inside. In larger boats the bilge stringer is often joined by ceiling which forms a nearly solid surface fastened to the inside of the ribs. Thwarts are fastened to the risers somewhat tenuously, the risers being only ½ inch thick, but, with standing knees holding the thwart down as well as supporting the topside through the middle of the boat, the whole structure is very strong, especially with inwale and rub installed. The breast hook ties the top of the hull together across the stem. The quarter knees do the same at the stern, providing strong connection between the sheer strake and the transom. The inwale and rub clamp all parts of the rail structure together, forming a beam encircling the boat, able to resist the forces of rowing and collision.

I'd likely use oak for the risers. Notice that at the transom the cleats that will bear the stern sheets across the transom are notched for the risers. These cleats could well be installed now. The risers are screwed to the ribs, staggering screw locations. Clamp the risers in place and fasten from aft forward. Clamps with 8+ inch throat are rare in my shop, but with a block between two ribs and a stick to the riser, a clamp over the rail will work as a long reach clamp. With the risers screwed to the ribs, beams can be installed between the risers that will support the fore and stern sheets. These beams usually have ogees or similar shapes cut on their undersides for decoration, symmetrical side to side as they are visible just under the inboard edges. They will be screwed to the risers and might bear also on ribs. A short cleat is also needed between the forward ends of the risers to support the middle of the fore sheets.

The thwart locations can be measured off the plans and positioned square to the centerline by measuring equal distances to each side from the stem. Some, not Arthur Spurling, notch thwarts around ribs but they should not touch the planking. The risers will not be plumb and, if the top of the riser is square, the thwart will land on the riser edge. With the thwart fitted, I like to run a pencil under the thwart along the riser and cut a groove along that line for more contact. Arthur Spurling left the thwart edges square with a little round relief along the edges. I like to cut a wide bevel on the underside of thwarts for a lighter appearance, starting inboard of the risers, leaving half the thwart thickness which gets rounded on the edges, for comfort. The thwart is fastened to the riser with a couple of screws.

Thwart relief and riser shape

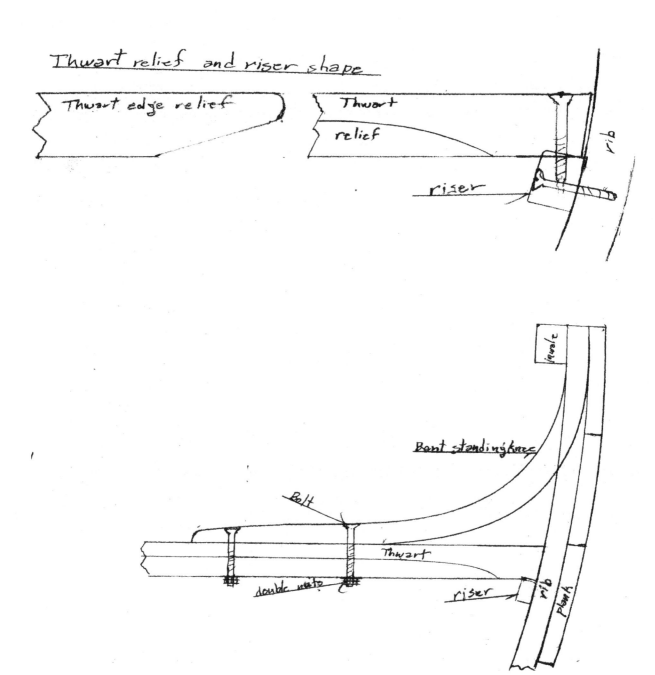

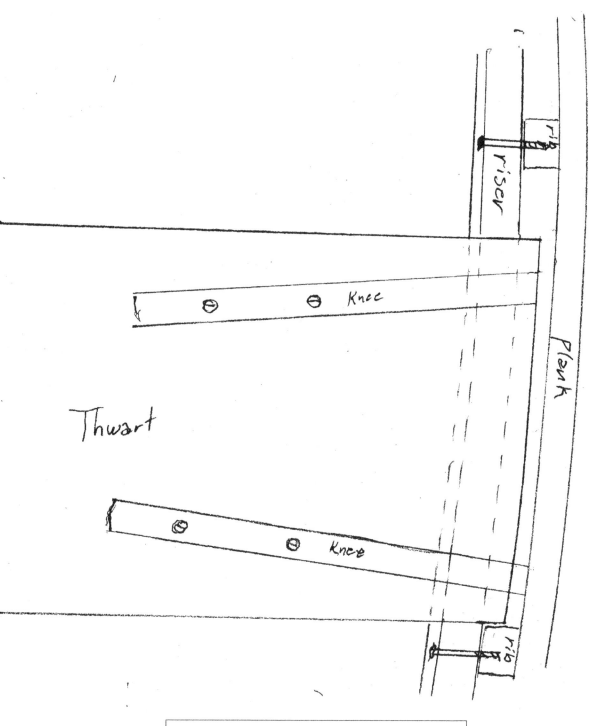

Thwart shaping and installation details.

Standing knees could well be installed now, especially if grown or otherwise solid knees, because these will be fitted and fastened to the planks. Arthur Spurling's grown knees extended around 9 inches from plank to tip on the thwart. Longer is fine with me as long as the arm on the thwart stands low. The standing knees come up behind the inwale. If they are solid knees they will be notched to 5/8 (the rib molded dimension, easily met if bent with rib stock) at the rail and if bent they should have that thickness for the inwale to clamp them at rail height. Solid knees are most easily fit before the inwale, bent knees have some flex so are not difficult to install with the inwale in place. With the thwarts fastened in place, even if just to the riser, the cross spalls can be removed.

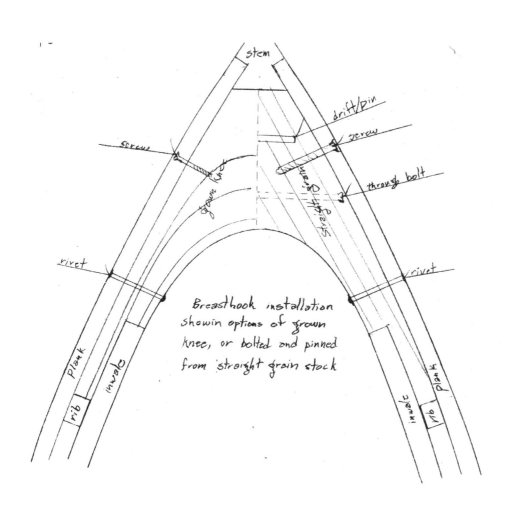

Breasthook installation showin options of grown knee, or bolted and pinned from straight grain stock

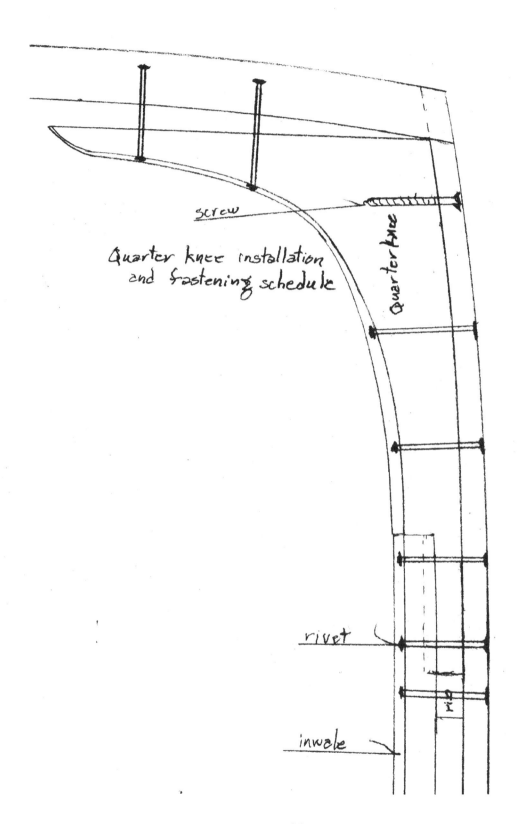

Arthur Spurling used a two piece breast hook on the measured boat, each side extending to the first rib. How he joined the halves, I don't know, they might be through bolted or just drifted together with short rod – in either case the bolt or rod can't be larger than ¼ inch. A grown knee is best, the angle between the arms matching the angle between the planks on each side. With the arms of the breast hook beveled to land against the planks, the arms are morticed to take the end of the inwale. The breast hook is fastened with screws to the planks and, when the inwales come, the inwale ends are fastened through breast hook and sheer strakes (as at the stern the inwales are secured in mortices in the quarter knees). As noted in the "details/scantlings" above, there is a quarter inch crown in the breasthook. Generally a breasthook will get crown matching the deck crown, in this case, maybe the transom. A cardboard or ply pattern with bevels can be made, or the actual stock can be placed across the bow and lines traced along the planks underneath; as the two sides might not quite match, cut square to these lines and then bevel to drop the breasthook into place to fasten after crowning.

The quarter knees are patterned and installed similarly to the breasthook. If riveting, go for it. Quarter knees can land level on the transom but better if canting up a little. Spurling's are grown hackmatack knees and, again, they reach the last rib, with a similar length along the transom. The mortice is about 3 inches long leaving the 5/8 inch rib molding for inwale landing.

The 1 inch x 5/8 inch inwales in Arthur Spurling's boat looked like mahogany but could well be oak or any relatively straight grain hardwood. Installing these starts with fitting one end with some of the rest clamped, usually the bow end in the breast hook mortice, and working along rib by rib (and standing knees if already there) toward the other end until it seems time (based on the flexibility of the inwale) to fit the other end to it's mortice. Little by little works best, cutting the piece to fit inside the quarter knee and making a final cut judged to fit tight to the mortice end. Tight is good but not the end of the world. To get the tightest possible fit we kerf, sawing along the seam at the joint, trimming both pieces so when the saw is removed the two can come together, tight. This is easy on one end, for the other end the inwale can be sprung out of position at the other end enough to bring the joint together as intended and slowly kerfed to the needed length and fit.

The 15/16 inch by half inch rub rails are rounded slightly on the outside edges and run from bow to stern along the sheer, rounded off at the ends. They get screwed through to the breast hook and quarter knees, and to the sheer strake along the way. Called "rub rails", they are what rub against a float or wharf, or what gets bumped against at the dinghy float, protecting the planking. I tend to use oak or another hard wood. Harder woods show rubbing less, but these are essentially sacrificial and any wood could be used. Again, Spurling's rub rails looked like mahogany. Many will cover the rub rail with protective materials, and many will insist that their boat never touch anything, but in my world things happen whatever one says. As sacrificial pieces, fasten the rubs with longer screws into the breasthook and quarter knees, and with short screws into the sheer strakes. Where there is blocking under the row lock pads longer screws can give more secure hold.

Now for the bow and stern sheets. "Stern sheets" is the seat or platform in the stern of a boat, but why? The Oxford dictionary defines "sheets" as "The space at the bow or stern of an open boat". The etymology gives Old English scēata meaning the lower corner of a sail, which fits with the shape of these spaces in the double ended open boats of old English and Norse times as well as the shape of a platform or seat fit in those spaces. The stern sheets in a transom boat like the Spurling rowboat is a truncated triangle while the fore sheets is close to a full triangle. For best support as well as looks, these seats are laid out in a fan shape. A full pattern can be made for layout purposes but it is also possible to do the layout in place, working from the outside in with measurements marked on the cleats and beams already in place.

Now would be a good time to turn the boat over again to fair and caulk. The boat still needs floor boards inside, and the oak shoe under the keel, as well as rowlocks and pads, and other hardware shown on the details/scantlings list. The shoe gets fastened from the inside between stem and skeg, so must be installed before the floorboards. I say "fair and caulk first" to tighten up the hull and get a start toward finish which will start with raw linseed oil, but fairing comes before oil.

Molds out of the way and rail structure complete, the upturned boat can now sit on it's rails, or on the seats, if lower works better; comfort for planeing and sanding should determine how the hull is supported, and can be changed as fairing continues. Fairing might start by working the cutwater into the stem, from square to wedge shape. The brass half oval band down the stem is half an inch wide, so that span must be left square down the center of the stem, flaring out at the bottom of the stem where it butts to the shoe. With lines drawn for band position, the corners are planed away between the rabbet and the lines on the stem face. A power planer is a great help in removing much of this wood but a sharp plane, spoke shave and scraper are best for finishing the job. Some adjustment will be wanted when the shoe is installed, before installing the stem band.

For hull fairing I find a wood bodied smoothing/coffin plane the best tool for the job, the quality of the old cast steel blades helps, but light weight and feel in the hand helps too. Where we find reverse curve a backing out plane will be useful. A slight concave spar plane could be used, but I find the smoothing plane is all that's needed, mostly. Like nearly all boat jobs, when one tool stops being satisfactory another one works better and soon there is a bench load of tools getting used. First make sure all fasteners heads lie below the half inch finished thickness. If in doubt, pull the screw and redrill, or if close just give it a few turns. This takes less time than resharpening.

The most important tool in fairing is the hand. You can feel more than you can see. Running the hand up and down the hull, you feel the rise and fall, the high points need planing off – always with the plank. Some people want to plane on an angle, up and down the hull, but the planks were backed out to the planned thickness and fairing is done to bring all the planking to that thickness, so we plane off the high points which are mostly lines along the joints between the planks. Your hand will feel where the plane needs to go. You start planing along the plank lines, the obvious high places, and then start feeling your way toward fair and smooth. Around and around, one side and then the other. The straight bladed smoothing plane can make the planks remarkably fair with the hand guiding the plane. Final smoothing is done with sandpaper or a sharp scraper, different woods respond differently to different approaches.

Good scrapers can be purchased but many have been cut from old hand saw blades. For hull fairing, a cabinet scraper with a straight edge and some flexibility is needed. Audel manuals say to sharpen the edge to a 45 degree angle and then turn the edge with a burnisher, the burnisher a polished hardened steel rod, sometimes triangular, sometimes round or oval. Better is a polished 90 degree edge with two edges that can be turned with the burnisher. The edge, square or 45, must be sharpened just like a chisel, polished edge to polished edge, for best results. The turned edge should cut a curl as it is scraped along the surface at around 80 degrees, if not it needs reworking. For fairing, the scraper is bent to approximate the hull curve as it is worked.

With the boat upside down it now asks to be caulked but first I'd like to start laying on raw linseed oil. This calls for my discussion of linseed oil. My discussion of linseed oil starts many years ago when I remember reading L. Francis Herreshoff saying his only job in his father's shops was applying linseed oil and that they linseed oiled every part of the boats. I haven't been able to find that quote since so maybe I imagined it, but I was frustrated by his failure to specify whether the oil was raw or boiled.

Years went by with this question hanging around until I read a book by a British cabinet maker who said that when they finished a piece of furniture it was placed in the corridor between the shop and the offices. There, raw linseed oil would be applied. The oil would be poured on and rubbed in with the hand, the heat of hand rubbing being a necessary part of the process. The oil would be rubbed over the whole surface until it shone and then the piece was left for the day. The next day the piece would be dull, the oil having been absorbed, and once again oil would be rubbed in. This went on day after day until one day the shine would remain, the piece was finished. So then I was convinced it was raw oil used at the Herreshoff Manufacturing Company, however circumstantial the evidence. I thought this important but was not totally clear what to do with this information.

One problem I had with my old boats was the paint always cracked and peeled, so I had to sand, fill, and paint every year. I used all kinds of yacht enamels seeking a solution to this expensive exercise, they all seemed to be the same. Not that the whole paint job peeled off, just enough so it didn't seem right to leave it. Then one year when the WoodenBoat Show was in Newport there was a display of Allbeck Linseed Oil paint. I was busy the whole show but the last day, when everyone was packing up, I finally went over and told my sad story of peeling paint. The man said, Where do you live? Marblehead. He said, they all say it's the weather, the wood's moisture content, but it's the paint. You need to apply cleaned, raw linseed oil to the bare wood and then linseed oil paint, it will last 50 years. The raw oil absorbed into the wood bonds with the linseed oil paint. Allbeck paint has no volatile organic compounds that evaporate away, it is just pigment with boiled linseed oil treated with a manganese siccative that accelerates drying from the inside out, keeping a dry film from forming over uncured paint.

One element here is "cleaned" linseed oil. The contention being that blackening of linseed oil is not a function of the oil itself but of proteins remaining with the oil after pressing. Told this by the man selling the Swedish Allbeck paint, I looked up linseed oil in the 1911 Encyclopedia Britannica and found description of a couple of methods for cleaning raw linseed oil, as though that was a normal and common practice. Interesting.

Since that meeting in Newport, linseed oil paints and varnish have been my choice and I am very happy with them. A couple of years ago, when we were hauling my boat out for the winter, the boat yard boss said to me, "your paint is cracking", seeing a little separation at the plank joints, I said, "that's 5 year old paint", he said, "you've done very well." Before starting to use this paint I did "wood" the hull and apply raw oil a couple of times. I mention the Allbeck paint because the purveyor taught me a lot but also because it is the only available genuine linseed oil paint as far as I know. It is like all paint used to be before paint production became a product of the chemical/petroleum industry, best of all, it is a great pleasure to apply, brushing out beautifully.

Then there came one more pitch for applying linseed oil to boats. I came upon a book from 1950, YACHT AND SEA, by Gustav Plym, sailor and boat builder, whose family had one of the most famous and successful boat building yards in Sweden. His discussion of painting is an extensive argument for treating the hull with many coats of raw linseed oil. Towards the end is this paragraph:
"I know that experiments have been carried out, which show that linseed oil can be of little help in preventing wood from absorbing water, the fact is, however, that during the last sixty to seventy years some hundreds of the best built boats in the world have been treated as described above, and they have stood the test of time in a way which no laboratory test can disprove."

Applying raw linseed oil is very forgiving. Brush, roll or spray, no worries about thick, thin, or holidays. Plym talks about 5 or 6 coats, all of which will soak in leaving a matt finish. Applying heat lightly when applying the oil will help absorption but is generally unnecessary. Linseed oil will solidify over time, will stabilize the wood, and reduce swelling as the wood absorbs water. It is also the best primer for applying oil based paint, later. For now, we are ready to caulk.

The boat is ready for caulking if the caulking bevels are all open for driving in cotton. What to do if a seam is closed? I have made reefing irons, for reefing (pulling) old cotton caulk out of seams, by heating a metal file tang to red hot and bending it around into a hook. Heated to red hot again I hammer the hook on one side and the other against an anvil, to shape the hook end, giving it a narrow wedge shape. Filed toward the inside of the hook so the point is the leading edge and the inside of the hook slightly wider than the back, the reefing iron is now a wedge shaped scraper that can be drawn along a seam to open it for caulking.

For a small boat like the Spurling, rolling cotton into the seam should be quite adequate, but a little driving with a caulking iron would be good. A roller should give good depth control, one big no-no in caulking is driving the cotton through the seam. I like to paint the seams with red lead paint and run cotton in before the paint is altogether dry, then to paint over the cotton with another coating of red lead, this holds the cotton in the seam and gives a good ground for seam compound that will be applied when the paint is dry. When the red lead paint is dry, any on the outside of the planks can be scraped off with a sharp scraper and vacuumed up. I have carved handles for rollers and center drilled a coin to ride on a nail. I have also turned a roller from hardwood with a bevel to match a caulking bevel. I have also used a roller sold in stores for rolling gasket around screening in aluminum windows.

Once again, the ideal plank seam is tight on the inside half with caulking bevel to the outside of the plank, but if not ideal the seam must not be more open on the inside than the outside for the caulking to hold.

Caulking cotton comes in two forms, balls of wicking and sleeves of loose strand cotton. Rolled or driven, straight or looped, the cotton strands fed into the seam must be sized to the width of the seam. For a boat like the Spurling I expect the seams to be tight on the inside with a narrow caulking bevel so rolling in cotton wicking is the best way to go, quick and good. If you have loose strand cotton, it needs to be separated into thin strands and twisted to match the bevel width and then driven in with roller or iron. Caulk the plank seams first leaving little tails at the hood ends. When all the plank seams are done, then caulk the transom seam, pulling the little tails into the seam with cotton in the seam between the transom and the stern post, caulk right around from rail to rail. At the bow, the garboard seam caulking is continued to the sheer.

With the cotton driven in tight, painted over, and excess paint scraped off plank surfaces, seam compound is worked into the seams. Seam compound comes in white for topsides and brown for below the waterline, for boats kept in the water. These compounds come in cans for application with a putty knife. This takes some work. If the compound is too stiff it can be warmed to soften. When all the seams are filled a rag wet with turpentine or paint thinner is used to clean up the planks. Wiping with the rag should also cove out the compound in the seam a little bit so when the planks swell the seam will end up flush with the planks.

With the boat upside down and caulked, the strongback can now be removed and the oak shoe installed. The shoe is the same shape as the keel, a little shorter forward and a little longer aft. If the shoe is too stiff to easily bend to the rocker forward, it might have to be steamed but the bend is not much, 3½ inches in 6 feet, so the 7/8 inch shoe should bend on readily. Apply a good bedding compound like Dolfinite to the keel and start fastening toward the bow. Forward, the shoe is screwed through the keel into the stem heel, then from the inside through the keel into the shoe, making sure to use the holes from cleating the keel to the strongback. With the forward end fastened, bend the shoe down to the keel and screw with long screws through the keel into the skeg, moving toward the stern. It would be good to have one screw well into the bottom of the stern post, this is into end grain, so drill well for a long screw. Arthur Spurling rabbeted the shoe and stern post, installing brass bracket flush to protect and secure that joint. The forward end of the shoe must be planed down fair with the stem heel. After laying linseed oil onto the shoe, turn the boat over again to finish construction.

In order to install the center floorboard, cleats are needed for support. The center floorboard is the same shape as the keel, so the cleats must be just over 5/8 inch high to keep the floorboard above the height of the ribs at the edge of the keel. If these cleats are also used as backers for fastening the shoe, that would be better than having the screw heads pulling into the top of the keel. In any case, the cleats are most necessary in the room between the seats. The floorboards are ½ inch cedar. The floorboard shapes beside the center need to be spiled. The floorboards are screwed to the cleats and ribs.

Arthur Spurling put just one set of oarlocks in the rowboat at Mystic, probably for the particular client's intended use. With two thwarts, it is more common to have two sets, offering more possibilities for adjusting trim under load. The oarlock pads will be centered 12 inches aft of the thwarts to center the oarlocks there. Spurling's pads are 8½ inches long. They could be a little longer, but should all be pretty much the same. They should come out nearly flush with the inwale on the inside and cover the inside of the rub. This is an open rail boat and blocking should be fastened between the ribs under the oar lock pads. Cut offs from rib stock work well for this blocking. The look of the pads is much improved with a taper or ogee at the ends. Arthur Spurling used oarlocks that are no longer available, so, for the locks available, I would mortice for the plate and drill through for the sleeve that will carry the oarlock shank. Before installing the sockets, oil the inside of the boat with more raw linseed oil and apply bedding compound in the socket mortice. If possible, bolt the socket through the blocking.

A ring for the painter, the plate protecting the skeg, and the stem band are now the only remaining items to be installed, and it is a matter of choice whether to install them before or after paint and varnish. The plate protecting the aft end of the shoe is let in with a shallow mortice, to be flush, and turned up the stern post, so it should be installed before painting. A painter ring and the stem band might well wait.

Dories typically had holes drilled through the sheer planks for a painter to pass through and bear against the stem. Many boats have had holes through the stem for painter connection and some have a ring set behind a stem band on the face of the stem. I once had a neighbor, whose grandfather was a boat builder, ask me to look at the frame of a dinghy hanging in her shed. It was a Herreshoff artifact, but what I found most interesting was the hardware, lifting eyes, painter ring and oarlock sockets. After that I looked at Herreshoff dinghies at Mystic and the Herreshoff Museum, to check on their hardware, and found only the oarlock sockets consistently the same pattern. Clearly intended use and materials at hand played a part in setting up a boat in the Herreshoff shops, as well it might for us today, unless we are making an accurate reproduction of a particular vessel.

With your boat essentially complete, now it's time for finish, that is paint and varnish. There is the line attributed to Nathaniel Herreshoff, "A boat should be white or black, and only a damn fool would paint it black". The point of painting a boat white is temperature, to minimize heating the wood underneath. For the seats in a rowboat this can be a serious consideration when you go to sit, unless the seats are a light colored wood, for topside planking a light color helps keep the planks from shrinking.

In his 1910 book, YACHT CRUISING, Claud Worth says this of the tender he had built for his yacht FOAM. "When it was finished, a gallon of linseed oil (not boiled oil) was poured into it. Each day the boat was moved about so that the oil soaked into every part of it. At first the boat leaked a little. But it soon "took up" just as if it had been soaked in water, and with the advantage that it did not open again when the oil dried. In the course of two or three weeks the oil penetrated the planking and hung like little beads of dew on the outside. Then the superfluous oil was mopped out and the boat was stood up on end to dry. The oil made the plank translucent, so that the shadow of one's hand could be plainly seen through the wood. Wood treated in this way becomes very tough and is quite waterproof. In about a fortnight it appears to be dry, and is quite ready for use. But two or three months are required for the oil to become oxidized throughout the whole thickness of the wood. A coat of varnish then gives a fine hard surface. If the varnish is put on too soon the oil lifts it in little blisters. But the wood is quite able to take care of itself without additional protection. This little dinghy never was varnished during FOAM's lifetime." This dinghy was 8 feet long, lapstrake and planked with ¼-inch yellow pine.

So, I'm back to my pitch for treating your boat with raw linseed oil. In Claud Worth's time all paint and varnish would have had a linseed oil base. This is not the case today, with most paint and varnish petroleum or water based, enamels, urethanes, and epoxies. I think it important to know that none of these coatings keep water out. Water molecules, H_2O, are extremely small, one oxygen atom (the 8th smallest atom) and two hydrogen atoms (the smallest) making up the molecule. Boats sitting and moving in water have their under water parts under pressure, the water bearing them up, and any coating, like the wood surface, is a semipermeable, maybe permeable, membrane, allowing water through when under pressure. Wood also absorbs water through most coatings out of the air so permeable may be correct.

Paint or varnish, the choice may first be aesthetic, having a boat you like to look at in every way. Bottom paint, especially in salt water, minimizes drag creating growth and keeps toredos and other marine worms from burrowing into the hull. I say you will do well to lay on lots of linseed oil and then finish with linseed oil paint and varnish, but the main thing is to finish and get out on the water.

OARS

Ash oars, though generally I like straight grain spruce for the light weight.

Both the Spurling and the pram are rowboats as described and you need oars to row. There are a couple of places making pretty good oars, but even what I think of as the best can be much improved, and if you can build the boat you can make oars that are superior to any on the market. I am not talking here about racing sculls, which are likely to be carbon fiber, but about spruce or ash. Just as when I talk about building boats I'm not talking about glass lay ups or glassing, I'm talking about traditional wooden oars for fixed seat rowing. For a boat like the Spurling with a beam a little over 4 feet, 7½ foot to 8 foot oars are about right. One book I recommend to my WBS classes is Building the Herreshoff Dinghy by Barry Thomas, a Mystic Seaport Museum publication. Barry Thomas worked with Charlie Sylvester to produce this book, Charlie worked at the Herreshoff Mfg. Co. for over 30 years, mostly building small boats. The dinghies are lapstrake, but many of the methods described in the book are applicable to any boat building. The oar shown in the plans in the book, measured and drawn be Rob Pittaway, is 8 feet long with a 2 inch loom between the ovoid handle and the leather. From the leathering on, it tapers in the round, part way, and then becomes oval 1¼ inch by maybe 1¾ "square" to the blade, 3 feet below the leather, where the 33 inch blade begins. The 1¾ inch dimension of the oval becomes a spine tapering most of the way down the blade with the edges of the blade rounded and little more than ¼ inch thick. The Herreshoff oar was ash but those dimensions work beautifully in spruce too, and the spruce is much lighter.

If there is a trick to oar making, or any spar making, it is going from square to round, round here includes oval. The trick is to cut the desired dimensions square and then run a gauge along the square, drawing lines that will turn the square sections into eight sides. The gauge has pins at the ends one foot apart and pencils between at 3½ and 8½ inches, keeping the pins tight to the opposing square faces the pencils will scribe the lines. Planed to the lines for 8 sides, it is quick work to get 16 sides and then round. The blade tapers from 5½ inch width at the end to 2½ inches before reducing quickly to the 1¼ inch width throat. With the spine tapering to ½ inch at the end and the blade edge aligned with the loom of the oar, the mass of the blade blank is planed away, making a strong but flexible oar. Shape the handles to fit your hands with an ovoid shape about 6 inches long.

I like longish oar leathers in relatively thin but hard leather, oil/wax tanned split cowhide. If you bend this leather you see a whitish appearance caused by the wax being pressed to the surface. Cut to shape so the leather will almost circle the loom of the oar, the leather is stitched with a baseball stitch, double needle stitching started and ended with double stitches, between the stitches go from top to under with the first stitch coming always from the same side. Varnish the oars but not the handles. In use, tallow is the perfect grease for the leathers as well as the oarlocks.

WENCE THIS INTEREST IN BOATS AND BOAT BUILDING? AND ABOUT BEING FORTUNATE IN MY FRIENDS

In 1953 I was 8 years old, living in Minneapolis, Minnesota, with my parents, 10 year old sister and 4 year old brother. Our father was pastor at a big Lutheran church. One autumn day we went to Minnehaha Park and sat at one of the picnic tables, not to picnic but to talk. The question was, should we move to Africa? My father had been offered a mission job, if he accepted we would be traveling the following summer to Mlalo in the Usambara Mountains of Tanganyika. I was ready to see the world and, with my sister, said "Yes." So, preparations began. Told (falsely) that we needed to bring everything, 20 steel drums appeared in the basement, which our mother filled over the course of the next months. Then there were the 19 vaccinations scheduled, we were taken from school for weeks on end to the University of Minnesota medical center for injections, one week one arm the next week the other. Finally, the barrels were hauled out of the basement (one containing Mother's wedding ring, but which one?) and then it was our turn to leave, taking the train to New York.

At New York we boarded the French Line LIBERTE for the 7 day passage to England, of which I mainly remember the French dinner rolls, shuffleboard, and the ships wake on the dark ocean water. Coming to England was another thing: The ship was met by lighters 6 miles off Plymouth in a gale of wind, the gang way was lowered down the ships lee side, and those debarking met the lightermen. On the platform just above water level, the lighterman said "When the lighter comes up, step aboard". He took the hand offered and stepping to the lighter rail when the rail rose with the swell worked beautifully. With the lighters bringing us in to Plymouth, LIBERTE continued on to Le Havre.

After a couple of weeks in London, with many buildings still bombed out shells from wartime bombing 10 years before, we were off to Southampton boarding the Union Castle Line's DURBAN CASTLE for the voyage to East Africa, but while in London we had been told of a change in the mission's plan for us. One of their people in Dar es Salaam, port city and capital of Tanganyika, was sick and needed to leave, so my father was going to take over there, a lucky break for him and me. Leaving Southampton, the DURBAN CASTLE fought her way across stormy Biscayne Bay, and on, to make her first stop at Gibraltar. With a few days in that quaint British colony, we got our first view of Africa, across the strait from the top of The Rock. Then it was off to a nighttime stop at Marseille before a longer stop at Genoa, Italy. From Genoa we sailed past Stromboli in eruption, through the strait of Massena and on to Port Said, Egypt. My memory of Port Said is of the swarm of small wooden boats milling about our ship, rowed and sculled, a feature of all the harbors to come.

From Port Said, we went through the Suez Canal to Port Suez and the Red Sea. At Port Sudan, while DURBAN CASTLE unloaded using her deck cranes and local stevedores, we toured the area in a glass bottom launch, getting our first look at a tropical reef and it's colorful creatures. Then it was on to Aden, for a little look at Arabia, where a gale off the desert blew our ship and others out to sea, anchors dragging. Leaving Aden we steamed into the Indian Ocean through endless furrows of dark blue seas, to Mombasa, Kenya. In Mombasa we took another glass bottom boat ride around the ruined Portuguese fort and dhows at rest. After Mombasa came Tanga where we would have disembarked if we had been going to the Usambara Mountains, we did go ashore in a launch. Then it was Zanzibar and finally Dar es Salaam where, like all these ports, mooring was in the harbor unloading into launches and lighters, using the ship's gangway and cranes.

My sister and I had two weeks to get used to the view of the coconut palm ringed harbor across the street from our house. The house was built of stacked coral limestone blocks, plastered, with 18 foot high ceilings in the two big downstairs rooms and screened veranda facing the harbor. After our brief introduction to African city life we boarded the East African Railways steam train for the three day, 600 mile (that's an average of less than 10 miles an hour) ride to school on a plateau in the semi-arid middle of the country. For three years we had three months at school then one month at home. We arrived at the school with one other, bringing the student body to 18 – when we left after 3 years I believe there were 28. It was a mission school with most of us from the US or Europe but not all missionary children. Most of the students had more African experience than the headmaster or teachers, so we were pretty free when not in class or otherwise organized. We had our own activities, and then there were the mainly agricultural Africans with their crops and animals living in the village and in homesteads around. It was a good deal for us but then there was the month by the harbor in Dar es Salaam coming up.

    For three years we had our one month vacations in Dar. In that time the harbor was always there across the street from our house, past the coconut palms and dugouts on the beach, dhows sailed in on the monsoon, yachts raced out of the yacht club, small boats went back and forth, and ships came and went. After a few years a deep water dock was created and a tug boat arrived to work the ships to and from the wharf. After three years my sister had to go to high school, this one in Kenya with a different term/vacation schedule. To have the family together more than a month a year, our parents ordered the Calvert Education System for my brother and me, keeping us in Dar for the last year in Africa. Our mother had taught school before marriage and taught my brother 3rd grade. I was in 7th grade and taught myself. The course came with books and lesson plan. My program was, do the days work and get out on the town, which much of the time meant hanging around the waterfront watching the boats at work and play.

    We left Africa by airplane in 1958 for one year in Minneapolis before my father became pastor at a church in Warwick, Rhode Island. Our house was on a pond but Narragansett Bay was less than a mile away. We had a plywood pram for rowing on the pond, I had friends in high school who were clammers, others I knew sailed, but it wasn't until I graduated that I started sailing. I got a summer job before starting college as counselor at a day camp. I guided 15 to 24 7 year olds through the camp activities. When the camp brought out it's little fleet of Beetle Cats, they wanted the boats sailed around the point into the next bay and asked if I could sail one with a couple of campers, "Sure." Working with wind and tide we made our landing. Later one of the sailors running that part of the camp program said to me, "You know how to sail." That was nice. Then another friend working at the camp said his brother had a Sailfish (a lateen and daggerboard rigged surfboard) he could use, but he wanted me to run the boat. We put the Sailfish on the top of his 1949 Chrysler, put it in and sailed up and down the west passage of Narragansett Bay. We also sailed in the regattas out of his family's yacht club, the only boat in our class. The next three years, when I was home from college, friends of ours on the pond had a sailing dinghy they said I could use. Good fun.

I just always liked boats, crossing oceans in the ships, watching boats of all kinds, moored and under way, and the smaller boats were always wooden. I also always seemed to be a student of structure, from the flat roofed mud and wattle homes of the people around our school in Africa to proofs in algebra. I had been living in a house in western Massachusetts that might have been built as early as 1750. It was a plank house with chestnut planks mortised into pine beams, horizontal beaded pine boards nailed inside the planks for structure and interior finish, clapboards outside for walls almost 4 inches thick of wood. Pine beams connecting the front and back walls are supported by pine planks that form the dividing wail through the middle of the house, except for the massive 3 fireplace chimney in the middle. That house is a study in simple effective structure. I was doing carpentry, mostly house building, when a couple of friends bought plans for the Maxwell Cutter from then new WoodenBoat magazine. Looking at those plans and seeing how the boat was put together, I knew that is what I wanted to do. My friends never built that boat but I started reading everything I could find about boats and boat building, and building my tool collection and skills toward building boats, wooden boats.

I was often in Marblehead, Massachusetts, visiting, looking at the ocean and the boats. One day, driving out of town, there was a boat in a driveway that hadn't been there before. The head of the stem had been cut off, cutting right into the planks, but the boat was beautiful. The boat was covered and the covers rotted off over the next few years, until the day came when there was a For Sale sign nailed to the bow. After talking to the owner, I bought the boat with the help of friends, then I had to find a place to work on it. I tried with

Linc Hawkes who lived and worked next to Redd's Pond, but the best I could get was "it might be possible". So I went to the Marblehead Trading Company boatyard and found Ralph Anderson sitting on a fork lift. I said I had bought that boat and needed a place to rebuild it. I was there with my friend. He looked at us for a moment, back and forth, then he said "I looked at that boat. If you strip her to wood, we will do the structural work and you can do the rest." He gave a price I knew was good so that is the way it went.

The former owner of the boat said it was a Dark Harbor built in 1929 in Boothbay, Maine. I talked to the Rice Bros. relatives and Sonny Hodgdon who said, "between 1928 and 1935 we built no boats under 85 feet." Finally I talked to Maynard Bray, of WoodenBoat magazine. After a few moments he said, "Where are you?" then, "Where was it?" then, "Was it blue?" (she was white but had blue paint underneath) then "Did it have an engine with the prop to port?" then, "That is WATER WITCH, #5 of the Winter Harbor knockabouts, built by Burgess and Packard in Marblehead in 1906, I knew her when she was blue and in Portsmouth, NH." I sold that boat when done, breaking even, learned a lot, and made many lasting friends. I think that was the last big project to get done in the old "mill shop" in the former Graves Lower Yard, now turned into a large spray booth.

One person I met while working on WATER WITCH was Bill Hawkes, Linc's older brother. The Hawkes' boys mother was a Peach (local joke). She had bought the acre lot by Redd's Pond to keep a little of old Marblehead alive. In the early 20th century a big old dairy barn that stood next to the pond had burned to the ground, leaving that lot vacant. Linc kept it lively while he lived there. In the 1960s, the people living across the pond wanted to build a small house where an old livery stable stood. The houses were too close together to move the barn to the street, so it had to be torn down or moved across the pond. The Hawkes brothers went to work to get this small barn moved. They built a cinder block foundation and had Frank (Topsy) Goodwin, famous local building mover, prepare the barn for it's move across the pond. Linc's plan was to skid the barn across the ice in winter, on Topsy's timbers, but when that was tried the ice started to crack and all was pulled back. Then Linc got 150 steel drums and built a raft onto which Topsy moved the barn. Topsy had his equipment on the far shore ready to winch the raft across but, before that happened, Gerald Smith came across the street and said to Linc, "There's no wind. Let's row it across." So, they put Gerald's dory in the pond and got a boy named Roger Smith to handle the tow line, secured the line to the raft, and towed the raft across the pond, Linc's brother Bill standing on one raft timber and a pair of ducks on another. A crowd watched from shore. Later Topsy's crew moved the barn from the raft onto the prepared foundation. Lincoln Hawkes was a man who could do anything, almost. At one time there was a sign on the barn reading, New and Old Antiques Made to Order. By the mid-1980s it was used by a fisherman for storing his gear. Many boats had found storage space around the barn and now that I knew Bill Hawkes I was able to find space there myself.

I met Bill Hawkes in the Lower Yard mill shop while working on WATER WITCH, after becoming his tenant at Redd's Pond I mostly found him in his basement shop in front of his big South Bend lathe, turning out signal cannons, large and small. From high school in Marblehead, Bill had gone to the Essex Agricultural School, wanting to be a farmer. Enlisting in the Army with the onset of WWII, Bill had landed on Omaha Beach on D-day, survived unscratched and made it to Germany by the end of the war. Back in Marblehead, he drove a school bus for a local school and worked as a machinist at H&H Propeller in Salem, MA, but mainly he built cannons and it was always fun to stop at his house to pay rent for my space by the pond, talking and watching him working at the lathe.

WATER WITCH had been built by Burgess and Packard in 1906 and when she went back to Winter Harbor, Maine, a man I knew expressed a wish to have a Burgess boat. (The original plan for the Winter Harbor knockabouts was lost in a fire so the actual designer is not known, but it was Frank Packard who had visited Winter Harbor to ascertain what was wanted and he had worked as draftsman for Herreshoff (as had Starling Burgess) so the design might well have been Packard's.) Visiting the boatyards on Cape Ann, I had seen an Atlantic Class sloop at Beacon Marine on Smith Cove in Gloucester, filled with rainwater. Burgess designed the Atlantic in 1927, the first one built for the 1928 season. They are slender, low fin keel racers with a big rig and there are still active racing fleets 90 years later. 88 orders came in after a season racing the prototype and 99 boats were ordered from Abeking and Rasmussen in Germany. The Atlantic was purchased and moved on it's cradle to a spot behind the Redd's Pond barn, where I built a tent frame for cover and was able to work out of a shack that had once stood above one of the town's beaches. After the Atlantic restoration was complete and gone, Bill Hawkes got the fisherman to move out of the barn and I was able to start working in the barn now adorned with the REDD'S POND BOATWORKS sign and another sign on an old piece from the Atlantic, Wooden Boats For Sale.

    I built my first Norwegian Pram behind the barn. Almost finished, Gerald Smith came down the lane to introduce himself but mostly to say that all the details count on an elegant boat like that. Specifically, I had put blocky oarlock pads on the rails and he said beveling their ends, or a little roman ogee effect would give finish to match the rest of the job. After that, when I had a question, I would often stop in to Gerald's shop to talk while he carved decoys. Gerald had been a yacht captain and boat builder. He had grown up spending a lot of time in his parent's kitchen listening to the talk of seamen.

    Gerald's father, Charlton, had been a boat builder in Marblehead, most famous for building the Burgess designed Brutal Beasts, the local boat of choice for children. Gerald told how his father would send him out to change the centerboard pins in these boats, driving out the old pin with the new, trying not to sink in the process. He also told a story about the Beasts from the visit 5 J-boats made to Marblehead in the 1930s. The skipper/owners of the big sloops had the idea of a race among themselves in some of the local Brutal Beasts. This meant talking to the youthful owners. The story was that T. O. M. Sopwith, owner of ENDEAVOR, called one of these young owners saying, in his British way, that he was Tom Sopwith and wished to borrow a Brutal Beast for a race to be held with the other J-class owners. The lad replied "If you're Tom Sopwith, I'm the Prince of Wales" and hung up. "I think that was Frank Scully", said Gerald.

One day I stopped to talk with Gerald and he wasn't in his shop. I went to the house and Gerald waved me to come inside. He had had cancer some years before that had been in remission, but now it was back and they said he had only a couple weeks to live. After that I stopped there every day. Some days he was in no condition for visiting but most days we talked about boats and voyages. One day he was in his hospital bed downstairs and I could hear from the kitchen that he had visitors talking to him about local politics. When he saw me through the passageway he called out, "Come in, Thad, let's tell sea stories." One day, stopping to visit, Gerald's son, Lyman, came out and said his father was having a bad day, but the night before he talked for hours in his sleep, reciting the recipe for fish chowder and instructions for navigating into harbors. "He has so many stories to tell", said Lyman. Another day I was there with Lee Van Gemert and another man talking with Gerald when Gerald drifted off to sleep. We three stood there looking at Gerald, talking quietly. Somehow in our talk the subject of Coast Guard personnel came up, many of them from the Midwest or other places with no seafaring experience. Then, Gerald woke up and started talking. He named an old Marblehead sea captain, saying "he signed up in the Navy and went to Portsmouth for induction and training. This man as a boy had gone to sea with the fishing fleet. Part of their Navy training was at sea in a ship where the recruits were each given a turn at the helm. When this Marbleheader took the wheel he worked to leave a straight wake. The officer said, "You've done this before!" Later, they were at Vicksburg taking on prisoners. When he thought about how the ships crew was far outnumbered by the prisoners they were taking aboard, he was a little scared. He had had good relations with the ships doctor to whom he expressed his concern. Later he was notified that he was wanted in the Captains quarters. Not knowing if he was in trouble, he went to find the doctor and the captain waiting. The doctor said, "tell the captain what you told me". He did, and then the captain said, "I hadn't thought of that!" Then the captain called the steward and said to bring three bottles of beer. When the beer came the three of them sat at the table and drank their beers." That's pretty much how Gerald told that story. It wasn't until he said "Vicksburg" that it was clearly a US civil war story from

1863, the scene on the training ship suggested that he had heard what we had been talking about as he slept, and it also seemed possible that this was one of the oldest stories he had heard first hand. Gerald died not long after that day but months after the doctor said he only had a couple of weeks left. Meeting Lee Van Gemert there that day was a bit of luck for me as he became my chief consultant, with Gerald gone.

I was building the Beetle design No Man's Land (NML) boat as shown in Howard Chapelle's American Small Sailing Craft, working with my Marblehead friend, Rick Saunders. Rick had worked as a teenager in Hood's sail loft, like many other local kids. The Beetle NML drawing shows an iron shoe on the keel. I couldn't find the material in iron (not really wanting iron anyway because of rust, the NML boats in their day were hauled up on the beach when not fishing so protection was needed and rust was not such a problem), bronze strap was expensive and hardly easier to find, so I was thinking about stainless steel. Then I talked to Lee. Lee led me over to his shop and took a small piece of stainless steel out of a file drawer, showing how the stainless steel was eaten away on one side. He said this was a test piece from when he had worked in the pattern shop at the Fore River Shipyard. The test was to see what happened to stainless steel when moving in the ocean environment. The result is called crevice corrosion, degrading the material when oxygen starved, the face open to the water (oxygenated) was fine but the backside where it was fastened and unseen was corroded away. "I wouldn't use stainless" said Lee. Later, Rick Saunders said that when he was working at Hood's, Lee was the man Ted Hood sent when his boats were purchased by Arab sheiks, to teach them how to sail the boats.

Lee got his Dutch name from his father, a railroad man, but he grew up in the home of his Scottish grandfather, a boat builder at Lawley's in Neponset, Quincy, Massachusetts. When Lee was 15 he build a Snipe in his grandfather's garage. He brought that boat to Marblehead Race Week in the late 1930s, staying in William Chamberlain's boat shop for 50 cents a night. He went to the Massachusetts Maritime Academy and spent WWII as deck officer in a tanker. He said he had a very smart captain, when traveling the coast they stayed along the 30 foot depth line where German submarines couldn't operate without being seen. They were just lucky not to be blown up when crossing in convoy. Coming out of the war he taught at King's Point, the US Merchant Marine Academy in New York, writing a book on stability and loading of ships that is still in use. Married, he came back to Quincy, taking the job at Fore River. He was the man who made things, working with the engineers who designed ships and systems. Back in Quincy with his friends at the Squantum Yacht Club he bought an Indian Class sloop and continued his winning ways in the biggest class sailing in Massachusetts Bay. One year, after he had got the Indian fleet to buy Hood sails, Ted Hood was at the annual awards dinner. Ted came up to Lee at the bar and said, "If you're ever looking for a job, come to me." Not long after, the Fore River Shipyard started shutting down, Lee talked to Ted and moved to Marblehead.

Lee said that his sailing had always made his career. When he worked in the pattern shop at Fore River he would have his bag of sailing gear along and, regularly, the president of Bethlehem Steel, owners of the shipyard, would call for Lee and send his car so Lee could sail races with him. Then it got him his job with Ted Hood. Besides flying off to Arabia, Lee was tactician and alternate skipper for Ted when Hood's success in the Southern Ocean Racing Conference made his name famous world wide. Ted designed a One-Ton class boat for a trans-Atlantic race which Lee sailed and won with crew made up of Hood children. He won the 8-meter World Championship sailing with the King of Norway. He held patents for Hood Sailing Systems designs. Lee said to me one time, "I was in Newport (this was for the America's Cup in1962) with Ted on NEFERTITI, tied up over by the Ida Lewis Yacht Club when we saw the Stephens brothers, Olin and Rod, coming across the harbor in a Whaler. Ted invited them aboard and after a few minutes Olin said to Ted, 'I trust you completely, but you are making sails for your boat and sails for us and this can look questionable. What do you say?' Ted stood there for a minute, then he turned to me and said, 'This is Lee Van Gemert, I would trust him with my life. I will give him to you for the duration of the competition, he will set up a loft in Newport and make all the sails for you.' And, that is the way it went." For the 1967 America's Cup challenge, Olin Stephens' COURAGEOUS was fitted with Hood sails and she spent months in

Marblehead with Lee and a local crew testing sails, Lee ended up with her wheel in the room he called his museum. We went to Lee's 80th birthday party, one of the people who spoke said he had sailed many ocean races with Lee, no one was faster into his berth when off watch than Lee and, when he turned out, he always said something like "could that jib come in a little" or "maybe ease the main a touch".

One evening Lee was at a gathering in Boston, perhaps as a Massachusetts Maritime Academy board member, and was talking about having sailed Indians when the man he was speaking with said he had one in his back yard Lee could have. Lee wasn't sure he was up for having another boat at his age but his wife said he should just do it, so he did. He still had the trailer he had put together for his old Indian, so he put together the gear needed and got the boat. I helped him with some refastening but he got her looking and sailing great. He was leading seminars for sail makers at Doyle's sail loft and got a new suit of sails from Doyle. From being the biggest class racing in Massachusetts Bay forty years before, now there was no one racing Indians. The Indian is a John Alden design from 1921, the design drawn by Sam Crocker based on the earlier C. D. Mower X-dory design. With the old Indian home, Lee was walking across the Eastern Yacht Club lawn and saw his old friend, and former Indian sailor, Bob Campbell. Lee said he had just bought an old Indian. Bob asked the name. Lee said he didn't know the name but it was number 100. Bob said, that is CHEYENNE, built for my father. With her back in commission Bob and Lee sailed her down to the Squantum Yacht Club to sail in their Lipton Cup Regatta, honoring the cup given by Sir Thomas Lipton to the Massachusetts Bay Racing Association for Indian Class competition. Then, I sailed with them in the Crocker Memorial Race out of Manchester by the Sea, put on by the Crocker Boat Yard and the Manchester Yacht Club, and the Emperor's Cup race put on by the Marblehead Trading Company. Another year Lee entered CHEYENNE in the Crocker race but had to go to a family event, so Bob Campbell and I sailed the race and won, Bob steering his father's old boat for his friend Lee. Crossing the line, Bob kept saying, "I thought I'd tank! I thought I'd tank!" Lee and Bob brought CHEYENNE to Squantum one more time to sail for the Lipton Cup, this time I went down to sail with them, in gale force conditions. There was another Indian present, but they broke a shroud on the way to the start, so Lee, Bob and I sailed the race around Quincy Bay just for the fun of it.

Lee was the best person to sail with, as he was a great person to talk over technical questions, always positive and knowledgeable, with helpful suggestions based on long experience. He knew how to make a sailboat go. In 2000 he went to New Zealand for the America's Cup competition. When he came back, we were sailing CHEYENNE in the harbor one day when the racing fleets were heading out, including the Vipers. Lee said that when he was in Auckland he had sailed a race with the Viper designer and they had finished ahead of the fleet ahead of them. I was not surprised. When Lee got Cheyenne, it was his wife's encouragement that got him to make the move. When he had just started working on Cheyenne, we were walking our little dog past Lee's house and stopped in. We sat at the table with Lee and Marjorie, and our dog Bert jumped into another chair. Marjorie said it was fine for him to stay there. Then they told us that just the day before Marjorie had been to the doctor for a pain in a joint and been told she had leukemia, and only had a few more days to live. Sadly, this was true. Lee said after she died, "She was my only girl." I thought it possible that Marjorie had some inkling of her disease and knew Lee would need the boat. I know CHEYENNE gave him a lift, to think about, work on and sail. He did sell her when he thought he had accomplished what he could with her but he kept visiting and sailing with friends. One day he said he had a growth in his bladder and the doctors said it was safer to take it out than to do a biopsy, so he went in hospital for the operation. He had been on blood thinners and was taken off that for surgery. The operation went well, they said, but on the point of being released he had a massive stroke, leaving him paralyzed. Brought home, we visited him. He couldn't talk clearly but we spoke and then he reached up, pulling my head down, he kissed me. It was so nice. I think of that kiss like one day talking to Gerald Smith in his shop. Gerald was a lifelong Republican and had a picture of himself with old president Bush tacked on the sail he used for a wall in his shop. I am sure he saw my eyes glance at the picture when he said, "We don't agree about everything but I like talking to you, Thad." I have been very lucky in my friends.

Why am I so interested in wooden boats? I think a lot of it goes back to my time in Africa. Other than the steel ships, all the boats around Dar es Salaam were wooden, beautiful and interesting, but I think the experience of living on the semi-arid plateau in the middle of the Rift Valley had it's effect also. Everything there was very basic. The people around the school made their houses out of sticks and mud. The sticks were mainly from trees little more that shrubs. The mud was clay from the earth mixed with dry grass and cow manure. The roofs were flat, the houses rectangular. Around the houses were enclosures made of thorn bush, 10-12 feet high. In the night the cattle, cows and goats, were brought into the enclosure for protection from wild predators, hyena, jackal, leopard, or lion. The school buildings (there was only one when we came) were concrete block buildings with wooden rafter structure and corrugated metal roofing. All our water came from the roof, in the rainy season running from gutters into underground cisterns beside the building. For a while I had the job of sitting under the roof every day (it was probably 150F under the metal roof under the equatorial sun) while one of the local people who worked at the school worked a hand pump to lift water from a cistern into a tank under the roof so we had running water as long as the rains came in time. All the furniture in the school was made by local craftsmen who set up a shed next to the building where they turned out chairs and tables, windows and doors. One term we had woodworking class with the carpenters, working in their "shop". Then there was the plank house and the boat plans.

The plank house is almost entirely structural with minimal finish, most parts serving multiple functions but the whole is an integrated structure, almost like a boat. But the house only needs to keep falling water out whereas a boat needs to keep water out under the pressure of it's own weight. The boat also needs to move through water under control. Thinking about the integrated structure of wooden boats impressed the importance of boats on me, many relatively weak parts and joints producing a strong but flexible whole. I like trees and working with wood. I also really like the shapes of wooden boats, the way they look and the way they move through the water. When we lived in Rhode Island the America's Cup races were in the news and happening out of Newport. Somehow I got to know about Herreshoff boats and their history. Whenever I could I would drive to Bristol, on the other side of Narragansett Bay, just to drive past the site of the Herreshoff Mfg. Co. that closed down in 1945 finally, having been much damaged by the 1938 Hurricane. Many years later I was at what had become the Herreshoff Museum for a meeting attended by members of the Haffenreffer family, which had kept the HMC in business for it's last 30 years. Talking to one of the Haffenreffers, I told how as a teenager I had become enamored of the Herreshoffs and their boats but didn't know how or why. His response was "Because they are beautiful."

The beauty of Herreshoff boats is not just in the shape or the way they work in the water, but in the construction and method of construction. Nathanael Greene Herreshoff started designing and building boats for and with his family before he was a teenager. In business with his blind brother, who ran the business end, Captain Nat developed a building process that proceeded smoothly and efficiently from his carved model to a finished vessel. The Herreshoff success was impressive and their methods particularly interesting, but every designer and builder of wooden boats over the thousands of years of wooden boat building has had their own methods, each unique, but also developments and variations on what others have done before. Studying this long history of vessel structure, and being a part of it by building boats as they had been built in the past, has kept me interested and busy for the last 40 years.

There is also the sailing. I had to become a boat builder to get out on the water. Forty years ago I started building a dinghy based on Nat Herreshoff's Columbia lifeboat model. It became my row boat and tender, but is also a great little sailing vessel. After selling WATERWITCH I bought an Alden Triangle class sloop, a 28 foot Marconi knockabout (no bowsprit, jib tacked at the bow) beautifully balanced on the helm. Then I was offered an 18' Fenwick Williams catboat in exchange for building Gerald Smiths 17' variation on William Chamberlain's 19' gunning dory. (The Triangle sold to Finland, shipped with stock for restoration in a 40' container, where she was rebuilt.) I grew to like the catboat's gaff rig and the fun of using her weather helm for maneuvering as well as signaling time to reef. Since first encountering books on boats designed by Ralph Munroe, sharpies and round bottom sharpies known as Presto boats, I had been intrigued by his ideas and his boats, so I had built a 13' ketch based on Munroe's PRESTO, as a show boat. The mini-Presto sailed beautifully and capably, and did get me one job (building a Danish seine boat with hunting cabin powered by an Atlantic make and brake engine). Then a man contacted me, interested in a small cruising catboat. After he came for a sail with me, he made an offer and the catboat sailed away. This lead me to Albert Strange and his boats.

Albert Strange was an artist and boat designer, born in 1855 and died in 1917. While head of the Scarborough Art School in Yorkshire, England, Strange designed some 150 yachts, mostly small cruising boats. He was active in the Humber Yawl Club and wrote many articles on his cruises for the yachting press of his day, also a series on the design and construction of small cruising yachts. With the catboat gone I was looking for a boat. I had seen an ad for an Albert Strange yawl in Massachusetts but thought little about it until a friend stopped at my shop and said I should look at a boat he had seen in Salem Harbor. As soon as I saw it I knew it was the Strange boat. Including the 13' Presto with what money I thought I could afford, SEA HARMONY came into my keeping. She needed considerable cosmetic attention including cleaning wheelbarrow loads of growth from her bottom, but she had been very well built in England in 1937. SEA HARMONY is a 33 foot gaff topsail yawl and the last of four boats built for members of the Suffling family based on Venture, one of the last designs of Albert Strange. VENTURE, 29' 6", was first built to the design but finding the Suffling brothers wanted a boat more comfortable for more than a crew of two, they had the plan expended to 33'. N. R. Suffling wrote: "We were so surprised at the fine sea qualities of little VENTURE that I decided I could not do better than build from the same design, increasing the size to six tons." Finally I had a beautiful boat for ocean passages, I took her to shows and events until I retired. Seeking to emulate her designer, I wrote stories of our cruises for the Albert Strange Association yearbooks, now I have another circle of interesting friends.

Glossary

Batten: long, straight edged but flexible material for drawing fair lines. Straight grain white pine preferred but can be plastic or metal for particular applications. Pine can be planed to different degrees of flex as needed.

Beam: 1. Timber, square to hull centerline, supporting deck, cabin top or sole.
         2. Measurement of hull width at widest point.

Bedding: Thickened compound applied to joined surfaces to keep water out of the joint by creating a gasket, traditionally linseed oil with various thickening materials and sometimes white lead putty, now often rubbery materials.

Bevel : Angle cut on the edge of a plank to give proper landing with joining plank, on face of plank for lapstrake construction, on edge of plank for carvelconstruction.

Broad strake: Planks above the garboard up to the turn of the bilge, in round bottom boats

Breasthook: Structural piece connecting the sides of the hull at the bow, can be a grown knee, a casting, or a joined/laminated knee.

Burr: Stamped copper washer with small hole through which copper nail is driven before clipping the nail and peening to form a rivet. Functionally, a rove.

Buttock: Line in boat plans where a plane parallel to the center line plane (CL) intersects with the hull as drawn. Generally there are a number of buttocks indicated, drawn at spaced intervals from CL. In Half-Breadth and Body Plan the buttocks show as straight lined, in Profile they show as curved lines.

Carvel: Smooth sided hull planking, traditionally plank on frame with joints between planks caulked. Opposed to lapstrake.

Caulk: Cotton or other fibrous material driven into the seams between planks to seal out water, to be painted over and the seam filled with putty or some other seam compound, creating a smooth outer surface.

Chine: Line on hull where two hull surfaces meet at an angle.

Clinker: Hull construction where planks are fastened together with riveted or clinched nails "clinked" in the hammering. Lapstrake.

Deadrise: Describes the angle taken by the bottom planking from the garboard to the turn of the bilge in round and vee bottom boats.

Fair: Smooth and even curve in line or surface.

Floorboard: Material inside boat for walking on, makes up the sole.

Floor: Structural piece, wood or metal, crossing the keel connecting the two sides of the hull together, fastened to keel as well as framing timbers or planks on both sides.

Frame: Sawn timber more or less square to CL on which planks are fastened. Often set up before planking as building molds, often with ribs bent in between frames after planking is complete.

Gain: Bevels or half laps (often beveled) cut in the ends of lapstrake planks so the planks land flush at the hood ends, making a smooth joint with stems and transoms.

Garboard: Plank next to keel.

Hood end: Shaped end of planks coming to the stem or transom.

Keel: 1. Centerline structural timber.
      2. Often used for ballast extensions fastened to the structural keel.

Kerf: Width of cut made by a saw. To reduce friction, most saw blade teeth are alternately pitched to one side and the other making the cut wider than the blade behind the teeth, the kerf then will be the distance between the teeth on one side of the blade and those on the other.

Knee: Wood or metal structural piece with angle often near 90 degrees used to reinforce and support various boat parts, in use described as Hanging, Standing and Lodging, depending on orientation.

Lap: Plank edges joining one atop another in lapstrake planking.

Lapstrake: Hull construction with plank edges over-lapping. Bevel cut along at least one plank edge determines the angle at which the planks lie to each other. Traditionally joined along the lap with clinch nails, rivets or bolts, also sometimes glued.

Limber: Passage along keel inside boat allowing water to collect at the lowest point for pumping out.

Loft: Drawing boat plans full size to assure fair lines and determine shapes of backbone and building molds.

Mold: Form, sometimes sawn frames, used to determine hull shape.

Nagura: Stone used to raise slurry on Japanese sharpening stones.

Plank: Hull sheathing piece.

Quarter knee: Lodging knee connecting sheer to transom, in open boats will be fastened to the inwale as well as sheer plank, in decked boats will be fastened to beam shelf/clamp as well as sheer plank, usually bolted or riveted.

Rabbet: Ledge, groove or step usually in the edge of a piece of wood, also rebate.

Rabbet Plane: Plane, for cutting or trimming rabbets, with blade coming out flush with the side edge of the plane allowing shaving into a rabbet corner.

Resaw: Sawing edge to edge through a board or plank producing two matching pieces.

Ribband: Narrow board fastened bow to stern across building molds, usually following planned plank lines, to which ribs are bent before planking proceeds as ribbands are removed.

Rivet: Bolt formed from nail and rove/burr by peening nail shank over rove, usually copper.

Rocker: Fore and aft arc in boat bottom.

Rove: Washer for forming rivet, usually with cone shape.

Sided/Molded: Terms for specifying dimensions of vessel parts. Sided being thickness of stock as it is prepared for shaping, Molded being the shaped dimension as specified in plan.

Sheet: 1. Line connected to sail clew, often through a boom, used to control the set of the sail.
    2. Space, and platform often filling it, in the ends of a boat, stern sheets and bow sheet, the space shaped very like the clew corner of a sail.

Spile: Defining the shape of a curve, especially using one of a number of methods to establish the joining edge shape of a plank to come.

Strongback: Structure upon which boat molds or backbone are secured for building.

Thwart: Transverse structural element in open or half decked boat, often seating.

Transom: Transverse structure to which hull sides connect at vessel end, most often the stern but can be the bow.

Waterline: Line around hull at water level as boat rests in still water. Load Water Line (LWL) is the designed waterline for a vessel.

Made in the USA
Las Vegas, NV
26 December 2021